GUIDE TO
Better Business Writing

BOOKS BY MARY A. DeVRIES

Legal Secretary's Encyclopedic Dictionary
The New Century Vest-Pocket Secretary's Handbook
Legal Secretary's Complete Handbook
The Prentice-Hall Complete Secretarial Letter Book
Secretary's Standard Reference Manual and Guide
Private Secretary's Encyclopedic Dictionary
Complete Secretary's Handbook

Mary A. DeVries

GUIDE TO
Better Business Writing

NEW CENTURY PUBLISHERS, INC.

Library of Congress Cataloging in Publication Data

DeVries, Mary Ann.
  Guide to better business writing.
  Includes index.
  1. Commercial correspondence. I. Title.
HF5721.D35   808'.066651021   81-11129
ISBN 0-8329-0105-9   AACR2

CONTENTS

PREFACE   vii

INTRODUCTION:
ESSENTIALS OF SUCCESSFUL WRITING   1

1 AN EFFECTIVE STYLE   9

2 GUIDE TO CORRECT WORD USE   44

3 SPELLING, PUNCTUATION, AND CAPITALIZATION 73

4 NONDISCRIMINATORY COMMUNICATION   114

5 EFFECTIVE LETTERS AND MEMOS   128

6 BUSINESS REPORTS AND ARTICLES   152

INDEX   183

PREFACE

This book is a practical guide for everyone who needs to prepare written communications. That probably includes you because most of us communicate in writing at least part of the time. In the modern business world, success depends heavily on the ability to write effective messages.

Not everyone is ready to concentrate on the many aspects of successful writing described in this book. People who say things such as "I seen it" or "he don't know" should learn the basic rules of English grammar before trying to develop a more effective writing style. People who need to enhance their own sense of self-importance by putting down others should learn the basic rules of common courtesy (or visit a psychiatrist) before attempting to improve their writing skills. The *Guide to Better Business Writing* is meant for everyone else—managers, administrators, assistants, secretaries, instructors, students— anyone who must communicate in writing. Both professional writers and beginners will find the latest style information and other essential reference material. Beginners will also find easy-to-follow instructions for preparing specific forms of written communication.

The basic principle behind everything in this book is that business writing is a *practical* art. It is something you can do step by step, the same way you would handle another routine business matter. Effective business writing is a direct, clear, strong, and orderly expression of something you want to say to someone else. It is not a magical, mysterious phenomenon. Truly brilliant writers obviously have a special gift or talent beyond the skills of the average person. But anyone who is willing to follow the simple steps and observe the basic rules described in this book can learn to write successful business messages.

The "Introduction" summarizes the four main steps you should follow if you want to treat your writing as a practical, routine assignment:

- Organize your work.
- Research your topic.

- Write your rough drafts.
- Revise your rough copy.

Chapter 1 explains the six things you must do to develop an effective style:

- Use active sentences.
- Be concise and clear.
- Write strong openings and effective endings.
- Use specific and precise words.
- Avoid cold and pompous language.
- Delete trite expressions.

Chapter 2 gives you an extensive list of words that people commonly misuse in business writing, for example:

- ability/capacity
- among/between
- common/mutual
- defer/delay/postpone
- dissatisfied/unsatisfied
- practical/practicable
- reaction/reply/response
- viable/workable

Chapter 3 offers you a comprehensive style guide to correct spelling, punctuation, and capitalization, for example:

- Where to divide words with prefixes and suffixes
- How to use the semicolon to avoid confusion in long lists
- When to capitalize numbers and sums of money
- Which terms to abbreviate in business writing
- Whether to add s or es to make a word plural

Chapter 4 tells you about a relatively new subject for writing guides but an old problem—how to write without bias:

- How to avoid stereotyping racial and ethnic groups
- How to show respect for handicapped persons
- How to make your writing nonsexist

Chapter 5 shows you how to prepare two of the most familiar forms of written communication, letters and memos:

- How to capitalize on the *you* attitude
- How to choose an appropriate format
- How to set up the various parts of letters and memos
- How to compose actual letters and memos

Chapter 6 shows you how to prepare four other common forms of written material—articles, reports, proposals, and news releases:

- How to determine the best format and style
- How and where to research your subject
- How to make topic and sentence outlines

- How to write and polish your rough drafts
- How to prepare your illustrations
- How and where to handle the printing and production

More than one hundred people from business, industry, education, government, and other professions supplied the thousands of writing samples that had to be sorted and classified for preliminary analysis before this book could be written. Many of the contributors, including business writing instructors and other business communicators, offered valuable suggestions on content and presentation. My thanks to all of them and to the organizations that supported and encouraged the development of this guide. In response to overwhelming requests from advisors and contributors, I have included an abundance of actual writing samples, good and bad, and numerous models of different forms of communication.

In spite of all the suggestions, rules, and examples presented here, many aspects of writing still involve a personal choice. No firm rule exists, for example, whether you should write a professional title with a capital or small letter. This book recommends that you follow the trend toward undercapitalization: "The judge imposed a stiff sentence." But another source might tell you to capitalize *judge* in that sentence. If your employer does not have a preferred style in such matters, you can make your own choice. Either way, you should use the particular style consistently.

Above all, discard any fears or doubts you may have about your ability to prepare effective written messages. The *Guide to Better Business Writing* deals with all of the common difficulties writers experience and shows you how to overcome them. But keep the book on your desk and refer to it regularly, rather than try to memorize every rule in one sitting. That way, before you know it, many of the guidelines will become a habit, a good habit. The rest will follow, and soon you will inherit the many rewards of better business writing.

GUIDE TO
Better Business Writing

INTRODUCTION: ESSENTIALS OF SUCCESSFUL WRITING

Writing is a problem for many business people. To them, Winston Churchill could have been talking about business writing when he said, "It is a riddle wrapped in a mystery inside an enigma." They know that the quality of their writing reflects directly upon themselves. But the art of written communication eludes them nevertheless, and the more they worry about it, the more difficult it becomes. They forget that their principal purpose is to convey information clearly and effectively, not to be clever or witty.

Successful business writing is a *practical* art, and successful business people approach each writing task much as they would any other business activity—step by step. Such a practical, step-by-step approach to business writing projects includes four essential stages: getting organized, conducting research, preparing drafts, and revising rough copy. Following these steps will not make writing easy or enjoyable for everyone. But it will strip away much of the mystery and help you treat your business writing projects systematically and routinely, the same way you would handle other business assignments.

Getting Organized

Something happens when a business person takes pen in hand; the most astute, otherwise adept individual is often reduced to a helpless, frustrated basket case. But taking pen in hand is exactly what you should *not* do—not at first, that is. The first step in any business writ-

1

ing project, large or small, should consist primarily of planning activities. The easiest way to get started on a writing project is to *organize* your work. Plan ahead. Put the various steps in proper sequence and follow them, one at a time.

Many business people fail to get organized before they begin a task because the idea of planning and structuring something as small as a letter or a short, informal report seems too simplistic, too elementary. For those who stubbornly insist that this basic, systematic approach to a brief writing project is strictly fourth grade, look at it this way: well-organized, systematic procedures are automatically followed in most successful business activities, from preparing a budget to planning a conference. A writing project should not be treated any differently. Getting organized *before* taking pen in hand is a matter of common sense and good judgment. Perhaps few business people associate such preparatory tasks with writing because they mistakenly believe that for writing to sparkle, it must flow from the depths of some inner well of creativity. Unfortunately, this well always seems to run dry when it's time to write a letter or get out the monthly company news bulletin.

Getting organized is deciding what you want your message to accomplish, deciding to whom you want to direct your communication, and deciding what and how much information you want to cover in it. Some business people always begin a writing project by briefly summarizing these three components, and they keep these summaries in front of them until they are finished with the project. They do the same thing whether they are writing a two-paragraph memo or a two-hundred page report.

Assume you must write a letter. To summarize what you want to accomplish, you might jot down that you want to persuade John Jones to change the scheduling in his department to mesh with the release of a new product in your division. Or perhaps you must write a short, instructional report. To answer the question of whom your readers will be, you might state that your report will be directed to all supervisors and assistant supervisors in your West Coast assembly plant and your Midwest distribution center. Or say that you have to prepare a press release. To establish the scope of your information, you might note that you will announce the election of officers to the company's board of directors, give two or three basic biographical facts for each person, and include a brief comment from the new president. An important objective in getting organized is to help you clarify to yourself exactly what you want your communication to achieve, who is going to read it, and what and how much (or how little) you want to say.

Conducting Research

Research is the process of gathering and recording information. *Webster's Third New International Dictionary* calls it a "careful and diligent search." To most people in the business world, the process has broader implications. To them, it is a tool for efficient administration, the basis for critical decision making, and an aid to professional growth and progress.

Everyone conducts research, although not everyone realizes it. When you telephone local stationery stores to ask the price of 5,000 mailing envelopes, you are on a fact-finding mission, you are engaged in research. When you call the Holiday Inn to verify luncheon and conference room reservations so you can notify your staff about the next sales meeting, you are conducting research. Research is not limited to things such as report preparation or article writing. It is a daily function and a daily *requirement* for most business people. The more you know about research procedures, the better equipped you will be to handle your everyday tasks at work. For the business person who must prepare written communication, research is the second essential stage in a writing project.

What information do you need? Where can you find it? How long will it take? What will it cost? What is an easy way to record the facts you find? The answers to such questions are important to the business person who wants to do a thorough and accurate job of research and do it quickly. Research procedures vary greatly, of course. Gathering information to announce the appointment of a new marketing manager would not involve the same type or scope of fact finding you would use to prepare a report on new high-stress welding techniques. Research procedures for an awards presentation speech would differ from research procedures for a proposal to study shoreline erosion control. Yet certain principles apply to all forms of business research. A basic understanding of common methods and procedures will get you through most fact-finding situations.

Before you begin your research, a plan is essential. Assume that as part of the initial organization phase you outlined your problem. You decided what type of information you need, how much of it you need, and who is going to read your final product. At this point, some business people make up informal lists. First, they briefly state and define their topic or thesis. Under this general topic heading and thesis, they list all possible subtopics (and sub-subtopics) about which they want to collect facts and figures. Usually these subtopics become the subheadings you see in published material when one is preparing something such as a business report or article. Second, they list all possible sources of information for these subtopics. Finally, they list the various data-recording materials they will need in conducting their research.

You may think that most sources of information are well known to people in the business world. But surprisingly, many business people have no idea where to go. Frequently they overlook firsthand sources such as company files, co-workers, and company reports and other company publications. As a result, they sometimes repeat the research and writing that someone else has already done. Local businesses and other local organizations are an often overlooked, convenient source for certain data. Schools and research organizations have knowledgeable people to answer questions as well as an abundance of published and unpublished material. The federal government and local and state governments also have a wealth of published and unpublished material available free or for sale. To most people, libraries—public and private, general and specialized—are the most obvious source of all kinds of information. Finally, when fresh, original data are desired, you may decide upon direct observation or experimentation, or you may decide to select a sample audience and conduct your own survey. Available time, estimated costs, and your particular project needs will determine which of these sources you will put on your list. (Chapter 6 also discusses sources of information, including computer-assisted research and data-collection procedures.)

Not many people think about data-recording procedures. They assume that you merely go to the library or pick up the telephone or go to someone's office and take notes. But depending on the type of writing project you are undertaking, you may need special tools. For interviews, you may want a camera and a tape recorder to back up your note taking. Or you may want to devise a questionnaire form that you or your subject can complete. Perhaps you will also want to devise other special forms to use in note taking, forms that will simplify data collection and insure that you don't forget to look up and record something. Such self-designed forms are especially useful when you need lots of statistics in different categories from different sources. For general library research, you need a generous supply of 3- by 5-inch index cards. Each bibliography source should be listed on a separate card to make for easy alphabetizing later. Information too should be written on different cards and separated according to topic, again, to make for easy alphabetizing later.

When do you stop? When you have *more* than you need. Only then can you be certain that enough information will be available during the drafting stage so you can be selective. Otherwise, you may have to stop drafting and return to the research stage. Successful business writers try to avoid such unnecessary and annoying interruptions by following a basic rule: When in doubt, write it down.

Preparing Drafts

Say that you have organized your writing project in a logical, systematic manner, and that you have gathered *more* information for your topic than you could possibly use. The time has finally come to take pen in hand and write your first rough draft. This is also the time when many business people panic. Please don't. Remember, you are treating your entire writing project as a *practical*, step-by-step exercise, just as you would treat any other business task. Like the first two steps, this third step (preparing a draft) can be approached systematically too; in fact, it is best handled that way.

An easy way to prepare a rough draft is to build or expand upon your initial list of topics. During the research stage, you first stated your overall topic or thesis. Then you listed all major subtopics. Under each subtopic you listed appropriate sub-subtopics. In other words, you prepared a *topic outline*. For example, the general topic of this book is *business writing*. One of the major subtopics (chapter 1) is *style*, and one of the sub-subtopics is *active sentences*. To begin drafting, then, you need an outline that lists the key topics you want to cover in your final message. This outline should use one- or two-word descriptions for each subtopic and sub-subtopic. Be certain that all of these brief items are arranged in some logical sequence. Try to place them in the order you want to discuss them in your final communication whether it is an article, report, or proposal. If you are preparing a letter or memo or other short message, your topic outline will obviously be simple and short compared to that for a longer communication such as a formal report. But regardless of size, the arrangement of topics, and thus items to be discussed, should lead the reader at an appropriate pace to the desired conclusion.

Now you are ready to enlarge upon this topic outline by converting it into a *sentence outline*. To do this, take each subtopic and sub-subtopic and expand it into a single sentence. For instance, you could expand the subtopic *style* to say, "An effective business writing style can mean the difference between success and failure." You could expand the sub-subtopic *active sentences* to say, "Active sentences should be used to make a message direct, concise, and personal." Don't worry about writing beautiful prose at this stage. Simply expand each one- or two-word subtopic and sub-subtopic into some type of statement (sentence) that summarizes the main point you want to make in your final communication. (For more about sentence and topic outlines, see chapter 6.)

By now you've probably guessed the next step. Right! You take each sentence in your sentence outline one at a time, spread out all of your note cards and other research data pertaining to that item, and *quickly* write the other things you want to say in relation to each topic sentence. Don't worry about writing style or correct spelling or any other type of refinement at this point, and don't worry whether the additional sentences are in precisely the right order or whether the paragraphs break exactly where they should. The object here is to pull out of your research notes those facts and figures and ideas you want to have in your final communication and get them all down in rough written form under the appropriate sentence headings in your sentence outline.

Articles, reports, and certain other forms of business communication often include footnotes and bibliographies (see pages 154 and 170). Thus while you are quickly pulling facts from your notes and writing them under each sentence topic, briefly indicate the source of any possible footnote in the margin of your rough draft. That could save you time later. You may not use a footnote in your final communication, but it could be helpful to know the source without searching in case you want to double-check something or return to that source for additional information.

What you should have when you finish this step-by-step, outline-expansion procedure is an amazingly well-organized, though roughly written, unpolished draft. This is a good time to add footnotes (if any) at the bottom of each page, add a bibliography (if any) at the end of the work, and compile any illustrative matter such as tables and charts (see chapter 6 for details). When all of the information you want is written out, type it double-spaced. Now get set for the final step, the real mark of a skilled business writer: revision.

Revising Rough Copy

Professional writers like to say, "Amateurs write; professionals re-write." Everyone else likes to say, "Amateurs check things once (or not at all); professionals check things twice." Both remarks bear serious thought. Even common sense suggests that successful business writers automatically double-check their information, and they always revise and polish their rough copy.

If you made it through the first three steps of getting organized, conducting research, and preparing drafts, you are probably less skeptical about your ability to prepare effective written communication. But step four (revising rough copy) should not be dismissed as mere frosting on the cake. This step involves a lot more than putting in an occasional comma or correcting an occasional misspelling. In this stage, you need to evaluate what you have written; verify your facts and figures; correct all errors, from minor grammatical errors to misstatements of fact; flesh out portions that need more substantiation, more

facts, and more detailed explanations; reinforce material that is techni-
cally correct but sounds weak or vague or inconclusive; clarify (restate)
statements that could be misunderstood or not understood at all; eliminate irrelevancies and other wordiness; polish beginnings and endings
to catch the readers' attention and leave them with the desired impres-
sions; smooth out jerky, awkward transitions among sentences and paragraphs and sections; reorganize the order of sentences, paragraphs,
and sections if necessary; check for consistency in punctuation, capitalization, spelling, and tone; double-check for correct word choice;
put all accessory and supporting data (footnotes, tables, and so on) in
position and check for proper style; assemble the preliminaries (cover
page, title page, contents page, and so on) and the end matter (appendix, bibliography, index, and so on); and, generally, state and restate,
phrase and rephrase, until it all sounds just right for your audience and
your desired impact.

In case all of the above sounds like a tall order, it is! But you need
not turn aside in dismay. Like the other steps, this final step can, and
should, be handled systematically. Many business people make up another list, an informal checklist for punctuation, spelling, consistency
in tone and style, smoothness of paragraph transitions, and so on (see
chapter 6). All of the things mentioned in the previous paragraph
should be on this checklist, plus anything else you especially want to
double-check. Those who use this practical, checklist approach go
down their lists, one item at a time, and reread their drafts each time
with only one or two items in mind. Finally, at the end of their lists
after everything has been checked, corrected, and polished, they reread their drafts once more, this time from a total or overall stand-
point, and ask, "Does it all hang together?" If possible, always put your
polished draft aside overnight or for a few days before rereading it a
final time.

If you were to ask professional writers for advice on improving
your writing during this fourth stage, you would probably get a myriad
of suggestions. The most important areas of concern are covered in
chapters 1 to 6, and many of these problem areas (for example, spelling
and punctuation) usually can be mastered without difficulty. These are
the obvious areas of concern. But what about pitfalls that are not so
obvious? Most of such hazards are best overcome by cultivating a sensitivity toward other people. After all, written communication is sent to
people, not to horses or dogs or fish. In other words, be as concerned
about *how* you say something as about *what* you say to someone.

Presumably you send written messages to co-workers and other
business associates, clients, prospective clients, and the public in general. In business writing, the first commandment is "Know thy
reader," and the second commandment is "Help thy reader." Have a

clear picture of your reader in mind as you rephrase each word, sentence, and paragraph. The objective *always* is to present your message so the reader can quickly and easily digest it. The objective *never* is to show off and try to overwhelm the reader with your great intellect and wit. Chapters 1, 2, and 4 offer valuable suggestions for improving your business writing so the reader will gain the right impression and respond as you wish.

The quality of your business writing depends not only on your mastery of grammatical and stylistic matters but on the overall standards you set for yourself. If you have doubts about your ability to complete a writing project as carefully and thoughtfully as suggested in this last section, you might want to have an editor or some other qualified person criticize your final draft or even rework it for you. The important thing is to recognize that this fourth step is essential, no matter who does it. Only by adopting a systematic, thorough, and businesslike approach to this *practical* art can you fully experience and enjoy the fruits of better business writing.

1 AN EFFECTIVE STYLE

Style refers to the way you say something. Therefore, everyone who writes something, even a telephone message, has a style. The question you must ask yourself is whether *your* style is effective, because the right business writing style can mean the difference between success and failure in many situations. An effective style can sell an idea or a product; persuade someone to take or not to take a certain action; sooth a customer's ruffled feelings; and guide the flow of activity at work according to your wishes. A successful business writing style can help you become a more successful business person.

Most business people want their messages to be concise, clear, forceful, specific, and original. The problem is how to accomplish this impressive feat. They also want their communication to help them perform their other tasks more efficiently and effectively. Status quo in the business world is as bad as failure. Thus successful business people try to do more than is asked of them, and they try to do it better than others would. This policy opens the door to advancement, and that's the name of the game. To win this game, an effective writing style must become a crucial part of a business person's overall working strategy.

The first requirement in developing an effective style is to recognize that the burden is upon *you* to convey information so the reader can easily understand your message without risk of misconception. The reader is your ultimate judge and jury. But before the trial takes place, you must assume the role of reviewer and critic of your own work. To handle this role competently, you need a mental checklist: Have you used vigorous, active sentences? Did you edit your material for conciseness and clarity? Is your opening powerful, your ending effective? Have you selected words that are precise and strong? Did you rephrase comments that sound cold and pompous? Have you deleted trite expressions that make your writing stale and wordy? These questions should be at the top of your checklist when you evaluate your business writing style for its effectiveness. (Chapter 2 is an alphabetic guide to correct word use; basic spelling, punctuation, and capitalization rules are discussed in chapter 3.)

Learning to Use Active Sentences

If your writing seems listless, you may be using the passive voice too often. Although that sounds suspiciously like the start of a television commercial, many business writers do fall into this counterproductive habit unintentionally. Some people even prefer the passive voice, because they mistakenly assume it sounds more businesslike and professional. It doesn't. Too many passive sentences sound monotonous, wordy, and washed out. Compare these examples:

> *Passive:*   It is believed that the committee members should read this report.

> *Active:*   We believe the committee members should read this report.

Passive sentences lack the conviction, vigor, and emphatic tone of active sentences. They often have more words, unnecessary words, than active sentences.

You can easily spot the principal difference between active and passive sentences in the above example. The passive sentence uses a form of the verb *to be* combined with a past participle of the main verb *believe* (is believed). In this type of sentence, the subject is acted upon: it is passive. The active sentence, on the other hand, uses the present tense of the verb *believe*, and the subject *we* is the doer or the actor: it is active. As you can see from the following example, the pattern soon becomes familiar:

> *Passive:*   It is requested that you meet me in my office at 10:30 A.M.

> *Active:*   I'd appreciate it if you would meet me in my office at 10:30 A.M.

Again, the subject is acted upon in the passive sentence, and the subject is the actor in the active sentence. But this example raises additional questions; for instance, the active sentence is one word longer. Should the writer pick the shorter sentence? No, the opportunity to save one word hardly justifies using the passive sentence in this case. Besides, if space is a problem, the active sentence can be restated (a little more abruptly) by saying "Please" or "Would you please" instead of "I'd appreciate it if you would." Either way, consider the difference in tone between the above active and passive examples. The passive sentence sounds cold, stiff, demanding, and almost rude. Some readers might find it grating. But the active approach (which also provides the opportunity to use different words) sounds more pleasant and courteous.

The active voice is essential when you need to issue warnings or strict instructions:

> *Passive:*   This area should not be entered.
>
> *Active:*   Keep out!

Here the passive sentence lacks the force and sense of urgency needed to make these important instructions effective. But "Keep out!" leaves no doubt in anyone's mind.

Many people like to use the active voice in business writing simply because it sounds more like ordinary conversation. With the trend toward a friendlier, more conversational tone in business writing, the active voice is ideal. Observe the difference in conversational quality in these examples:

> *Passive:*   It is hoped that this shipment will replenish our inventory.
>
> *Active:*   We hope this shipment will replenish our inventory.

In normal, everyday conversation, people don't say things such as "It is hoped that" or "It was decided that." They say "I hope" or "We hope," or "I decided" or "We decided." The choice is clear for those who want their business writing to sound more like everyday speech. In the following examples too the active voice is preferred:

> *Passive:*   It was decided by the manager to close early on Friday.
>
> *Active:*   The manager decided to close early on Friday.

Although active sentences should be used whenever possible, the passive sentence sometimes comes in handy. You might have to expose a

problem that would embarrass someone if you used an active sentence.
A less personal, passive sentence might be a better choice:

> *Passive:*   The quota was not reached in the production de-
>   partment this month.
>
> *Active:*   The production manager did not meet his quota
>   this month.

Using the passive sentence to avoid embarrassment or accusation can
be carried too far. Some business people rely on the passive voice to
hide their mistakes, but it seldom works. Co-workers would probably
see through this passive, impersonal explanation given by a production
manager:

> *Passive:*   Because production estimates exceeded output,
>   an excess supply of raw materials has resulted.
>
> *Active:*   Because I overestimated our output potential, we
>   have an oversupply of raw materials in stock.

Some business people use the passive sentence to avoid taking a firm
stand. Often they are uncertain about their facts, or they fear being
proved wrong. Notice the obvious difference in degree of commitment
and assurance conveyed by these examples:

> *Passive:*   It is expected that sales will decline next quarter.
>
> *Active:*   I expect sales to decline next quarter.

Passive sentences that attempt to mask uncertainty are always weak
sentences. Good business writing is strong and firm. Passive sentences
are not automatically weak or vague. They are more appropriate than
active sentences when the doer or actor is unimportant or not even
known. Each of the following situations therefore is best handled in
the passive voice:

> *Passive:*   The group was formed in the 1970s.
>
>   Helen Smith was honored by the Clean Parks As-
>   sociation today.
>
>   The damage was repaired before the guests ar-
>   rived.

Some reports, particularly scientific reports, intentionally use the passive voice to focus attention on the action rather than the researcher or writer:

Passive: The metal strip was attached to the pole one inch from the top.

The fluid was heated before the containers were filled.

In business letters, however, writers would no doubt use active sentences:

Active: I attached the metal strip to the pole one inch from the top.

I heated the fluid before filling the containers.

The type of written communication you are preparing influences your choice of active or passive voice. Other factors described in this section are also important in making your decision. But when all else fails, your best guide is always common sense.

Deciding when to use active or passive sentences is only part of the problem. Most of the above examples show that as a rule, you can safely use the active voice in all sentences except when a specific need exists to use the passive voice such as to avoid embarrassing someone or when you don't know who the doer of the action is or when your material is highly technical or scientific. But the next consideration, after deciding on the active or passive voice, is to be on guard against any unnecessary shifting of voice. You should avoid switching voice from active to passive or passive to active within the same sentence. These examples reveal how easily such a shift of voice can, and probably does, creep into your writing:

Wrong: The sales film was so entertaining that it was enjoyed by everyone.

Right: The sales film was so entertaining that everyone enjoyed it.

Wrong: The pamphlet presents such a biased viewpoint that it will be believed by no one.

Right: The pamphlet presents such a biased viewpoint that no one will believe it.

Wrong: The honor was bestowed by the president, and everyone in the department endorsed it.

Right: The honor was bestowed by the president and was endorsed by everyone in the department.

or   The president bestowed the honor, and everyone in the department endorsed it.

Using active and passive sentences correctly in paragraph development and transition is important too. A careful writer will not switch voices unnecessarily from one paragraph to another. The following two-paragraph examples show how active sentences can brighten and strengthen a message; notice especially that the active voice sounds warmer and friendlier:

Passive: Special care is taken in packing your orders. However, every shipment is insured, and prompt adjustment will be made if your package arrives damaged.

Only quality products are offered. But items may be returned by you if desired, and your money will be refunded promptly without question. Your suggestions and comments will be welcomed, and our very best efforts will be made to satisfy you.

Active: We take special care in packing your orders. However, we insure every shipment and will make prompt adjustment if your package arrives damaged.

We offer only quality products. But you may return items if desired, and we will refund your money promptly without question. We welcome your comments and suggestions and will do our very best to satisfy you.

If your aim is to develop a more effective style, keep this general guideline in mind whenever you are preparing written communication: Use *active* sentences when you want your messages to be direct, concise, and personal; use *passive* sentences when you want your messages to be indirect and impersonal. Both voices, active and passive, have their place and both are essential in business writing. The problem is that business people too often use the passive voice unnecessarily. Learning to use more active sentences is a necessary step toward better business writing.

Editing Your Own Writing for Conciseness and Clarity

Have you ever had a friend who takes forever to tell a story? Sometimes you need all of the restraint you can muster to resist saying, "Would you please get to the point!" Some business people who handle their oral speech admirably nevertheless fall prey to this irritating habit in their written messages. Wordiness is a major weakness in most forms of writing, so it is not surprising that a lot of business writing suffers from this problem too. The question is what to do about it, and the answer is to learn how to make your own writing concise and clear.

Conciseness

One of the greatest gifts a business person can possess is a knack for simplicity and conciseness in business writing. Plain, simple messages, shorn of excess verbage, are much more likely to be read and understood correctly than complicated, rambling communication. Some business people are so busy that they refuse to read anything that appears too involved. They either skim it or discard it or give it to someone else to handle. If you want to be certain the recipient will read your message, make it concise and keep it short. Not all messages can be brief, however. The point is not to eliminate essential information; it is to present such information in as few words as possible and to eliminate the irrelevancies, clichés, and trite language.

Clichés are particularly out of place in business writing. Consider these sentences which appeared in a press release sent to a national magazine:

> Don Carter brings to our association a *tried and tested* background in economics. Many times in the past he has *vehemently opposed* wage and price controls. *With reference to* the administration's present policy, he has been an ardent critic, delivering rebuttals *straight from the shoulder*. Don promises to keep our association *abreast of the times*.

Many busy magazine and newspaper editors would pass over this wordy news item for one that required less time to make it suitable. However, here is the way it was rewritten for possible publication:

> Don Carter brings to the association a successful background in economics. He has frequently opposed wage and price controls and has been a frank critic of administration policies. He promises to keep association members up to date.

Notice how the elimination of clichés and general wordiness trimmed the original message from fifty-five to thirty-seven words, a saving of eighteen words. To a magazine or newspaper editor with limited space and limited time to rewrite material, this can mean the difference between using or discarding the copy. (The section "Guarding Against Trite Expressions," page 34, discusses ways to eliminate trite expressions from your business communication.)

Some words are simply useless. Business people are much too fond of words and phrases such as *concept, the fact that,* and *account for.* Thus you see sentences such as these:

> The overseas liaison officer said he agreed that the concept of apartheid is abhorrent.

> The sales manager devised a new strategy because of the fact that competition was increasing.

> A sudden outbreak of flu may account for the president's decision to close the school.

Such sentences should be rephrased to delete unnecessary words that weaken and clutter a message:

> The overseas liaison officer agreed that apartheid is abhorrent.

> The sales manager devised a new strategy because competition was increasing.

> The president may have closed the school because of a sudden flu outbreak.

Not only are some words and phrases unnecessary, some information is also irrelevant. Look at this paragraph from a memo sent by an admission's director to the president in a small college:

> I have spent the past week analyzing brochures for learning disabilities programs. As you might expect, some are good, and some are not. I believe that we should have a learning disabilities brochure for spring recruitment. I'm enclosing a sample of the type that would be appropriate for us.

Read the first two sentences again: "I have spent the past week. . . ." "As you might expect. . . ." Who cares? Did the president really need this information? The message would have been much more direct and forceful if it had started, "I believe that we should have. . . ." or simply, "We need. . . ."

Unnecessary words and phrases, useless information, inevitably weaken a message and expose a writer's careless style. Business people who prepare written material at work need to ask: Is this word necessary? Does this sentence say the same thing as an earlier sentence? Is this phrase trite? Is this information essential?

In addition to the trite words and phrases illustrated in the last section of this chapter, here are some examples of wordiness that should be edited out of your written communication:

advance planning (planning)

agreeable and satisfactory (*pick one*)

basic fundamentals (fundamentals)

consensus of opinion (consensus)

divide and separate (*pick one*)

first and foremost (*pick one*)

large in size (large)

in the year of 1981 (in 1981)

my personal opinion (my opinion)

quick as a flash (quickly)

the most unique (unique)

the reason is because (the reason is *or* because)

thought and consideration (*pick one*)

true facts (facts)

united together (united)

visible to the eye (visible)

worthy of merit (worthy)

The previous section explained how the use of the active voice can sometimes save words:

Passive: It is believed that the deal will go through.

Active: We believe the deal will go through.

Other introductions also contain unnecessary words and phrases:

Poor: There are four models available.

Better: Four models are available.

Poor: Due to the fact that the plane was late, we post-
           poned the session.

Better: Because the plane was late, we postponed the
           session.

Repetition, except for that intentionally used for certain audiences and
to make an important point, is undesirable in business writing:

Wrong: A souvenir paperweight, which is given to all pro-
           spective members, is sent to each applicant.

Right: A souvenir paperweight is sent to each applicant.

Conciseness must be the aim of every business person who wants to
develop an effective writing style. The best way to develop a knack for
simplicity and conciseness is to go through your rough drafts word for
word and ruthlessly delete any word, phrase, sentence, or thought that
is not essential. Some "excess" language is used by skilled writers for
effect. But the wordiness described in this section usually results from
poor judgment and a lack of good editing skills.

Clarity

Clarity is not always achieved as easily as conciseness. Many
things contribute to clarity: the logical sequence in which thoughts
flow from beginning to end; the success with which principal points
are emphasized and secondary points are subordinated; the smoothness
of transition among sentences, paragraphs, and ideas; the conciseness
of language and care in word choice; the pace at which ideas are presented in relation to the reader's ability to comprehend your message;
the care used in spelling and punctuation; and the consistency in style
and tone; and so forth.

Because so many factors affect the clarity of your writing, no single, easy rule applies to this problem. However, one question—clarity
for whom?—is easily answered. Business people need to edit their
writing to make it clear to the *reader.* Awkward, vague, ambiguous,
and incoherent expressions confuse readers. Although the level of
comprehension differs among readers, readability is important to any
audience. As a rule, simple, familiar words and short sentences will
make your messages more readable.

Sometimes it seems as if the act of writing brings out the worst in us. Business people have an irresistible urge to impress readers with their specialized knowledge and ability. To be certain readers won't underestimate them, they sprinkle their writing with a generous supply of profundities intended to leave the readers scratching their heads in awe. For extra insurance they add some fashionable expressions such as *shortfall, interface,* and *feedback.* For the benefit of the "slow" reader who still isn't properly impressed, the writer changes simple words such as *aware, begin,* and *use* to *cognizant, commence,* and *utilize.* What the writer doesn't realize is that some readers are going to be convulsed with laughter over this absurd, egocentric display. Others are probably going to toss the message in the nearest wastebasket. Most attempts of this sort to impress a reader backfire (for more details, see the section "Avoiding Cold and Pompous Writing," page 29). Good writing is simple, clear, and precise. Business people need to express their thoughts simply, clearly, and precisely to avoid annoying, boring, confusing, and losing their readers.

The following paragraph comes from an article intended for a company newsletter. The purpose was to get employees excited about the use of color dynamics to promote efficiency in the office:

> *Color dynamics* is the science of the effect of color on emotional reactions. According to psychologists, colors that render the office atmosphere dark precipitate an adverse response and tend to depress the worker. Colors that are too bright will produce a contrary reaction and may cause overstimulation of active behavior in certain individuals. The dark colors are believed to induce a reduction in worker efficiency, while the brighter colors are believed to effect an increase in efficiency through their characteristic of additional light reflection.

Many employees were probably so bored that they never finished the article. Others may have finished the piece without a clear understanding of what color does to people in an office. Restating the paragraph this way might have helped:

> Did you know that colors can make you tired, happy, tranquil, or angry? This effect of color on people is called *color dynamics,* and it's being used now in some of our offices. Psychologists say that people react differently to dark and bright colors. An office that is too dark can make you depressed. An office that is too bright can make you overexcited. Generally, dark colors decrease your efficiency and bright colors (which reflect extra light) increase your efficiency.

Writers who outline their proposed communication have less trouble with reader confusion caused by an illogical sequence of events. They usually draft their topics in the order shown on their outline, and presumably they iron out most problems in logical sequence while preparing the outline. Writers who use an outline also have less trouble handling primary and secondary ideas. When outlines list all subtopics and sub-subtopics, writers are more likely to emphasize the primary ideas (the subtopics) and subordinate the secondary ideas (the sub-subtopics) during the drafting stage. Considerations such as pace depend largely on the reader's ability to understand your message. The lower the reader's level of comprehension, the slower your pace will have to be to make your message clear. But some problems would confuse, or at least slow down, any reader. Notice what happens when a comma is used in place of a semicolon in the first example:

> *Wrong:*   We mailed second notices for invoices 0400, 0511, 0516, 0521, and 0522, and 0389, 0391, and 0399 require third notices.

> *Right:*   We mailed second notices for invoices 0400, 0511, 0516, 0521, and 0522; invoices 0389, 0391, and 0399 require third notices.

Sometimes poor word choice creates the wrong impression; the employee here was not handicapped:

> *Wrong:*   He was fired because of his disability to work under pressure.

> *Right:*   He was fired because of his inability to work under pressure.

Chapter 2 has an extensive list, with definitions, of words that are often misused, and chapter 3 covers basic rules for punctuation to avoid confusion. All of the suggestions discussed in this chapter and in chapters 2 and 3 are necessary for anyone who wants to develop a clear and effective business writing style.

Writing Powerful Openers and Effective Endings

To many business people the beginning and the ending of a message are the most difficult parts of written communication. Even when they get something down on paper, it sounds flat and unimaginative.

But they don't know how to repair the damage, so the message goes out, still flat, still unimaginative.

Openers

The danger is that if you don't hook readers in the beginning, they may not finish reading your message. Professional writers therefore often refer to an article opening as a narrative hook. The idea is to make the opening of any communication—letter, memo, article, proposal, or publicity material—so interesting that readers simply cannot resist reading the rest of the message. If you do not have a captive audience, it is even more important to have a stimulating, intriguing opener that arouses the reader's curiosity. But the opening is critical whether or not your audience is captive. In a business letter, for instance, the opening often creates the first impression a reader receives of you and the organization you represent. (See chapter 5, "Effective Letters and Memos.")

Good openings accomplish two things: They arouse reader interest in your message and introduce the topic and purpose of the communication. How much detail you include in your introduction depends upon how much your readers know about the topic. Regardless of the amount of detail you use, the opening must lead readers into the body of the message. A separate opening discussion that is only indirectly related to the discussion in the body of your message will confuse readers and encourage them to speculate without guidance. A good opening does the opposite: It guides readers mentally where you want them to go.

Some people love to tell anecdotes, and that's good. But opening your written communication with an amusing story that has no relation to the topic and then shifting directly into the body of the message makes no sense. On the other hand, if you can find an anecdote that relates intelligently to your topic, that's another matter. Say that you have to prepare an article on the hazards of driving a taxi. An opening line about cabdrivers such as this might be appropriate:

> It must be great to be a cabdriver—imagine being able to go to work every day in a taxi! Or is it really so great? Right now, while you are reading this, at least one cabdriver in our city is being robbed at gunpoint. Driving a taxi has become a hazardous occupation.

The anecdote should not be so long that readers sense a delay before they learn the topic and purpose of the communication. It must be not only related to your topic but in good taste. A hilarious opening followed by the gory details of a fatal accident would offend and shock most readers.

Some writers like to begin with an intriguing teaser. Say that you are preparing some publicity material on your company's new mechanical household helper. You might try this:

> You've head about the thousands of robots that handle assembly duties for American and Japanese auto manufacturers. For years women have been urging someone to create a similar robot to help them around the house, and for years social scientists have been debating how such a device would affect the family unit, for better or for worse. Futuristic Innovations believes it would change American households for the better. That is why we would like to have you meet Harold, our new mechanical household helper.

Business people who are preparing in-house communication often use revealing statistics or new findings to interest the co-workers for whom the message is intended.

> The number of employees who worked more than twelve hours a week overtime doubled last month over the previous month. Although special circumstances caused the increase to be unusually high, I believe we need to add new permanent employees in two departments.

Openers for messages that are in response to something or some request need to explain the purpose of the communication. When the purpose is obvious to the reader, a brief reminder is sufficient. If the communication about employee overtime was in response to someone's request for a study in this area, you might change the first sentence to read:

> Our study of the changing pattern of overtime showed that . . .

Formal reports usually require more formal, and possibly more detailed, introductions. If the report contains a lot of specialized or technical information, you may want to state your thesis, describe your investigation and its scope, define unfamiliar terminology, and summarize (introduce) the report's findings or proposals. But the need for a more formal, detailed introduction is not meant as an excuse to be long winded. As quickly as possible, the introduction should guide the reader into the body of the message.

Business people should not overuse definitions and quotations for openers. But some definitions might be interesting indications of or insights into your message, and some quotations might create exactly the impression you want. The following type of quotation is common in business articles, conference papers, and news releases:

> "Consumers find it difficult to judge whether the best exterior fabric for luggage is nylon, cotton, vinyl, or plastic," according to Consumer Studies President R. V. Fields. This problem led us to conduct a series of studies. . . .

Questions are a favorite opener for many people. Advertisements will give you lots of ideas for opening questions. These queries are only a few found in one magazine:

> Would you like to win free gas for one year?
>
> How can you get your hands on the small-car comfort option that helps pay for itself?
>
> Can being in the right place at the right time launch an executive into the top spot?
>
> Would you believe . . . a solar fabric that keeps you warm down to 30° below zero?

Endings

The ending is your last chance to reinforce the points you made in the body of your message, your last opportunity to be certain the readers go away with the impression you want them to have. It would be a mistake to stop abruptly after the last point in the body of your message or to do no more than say, "That's all, folks." A good rule is never to leave your readers hanging. Of course this is no time for a long-winded commentary either.

Endings must be just as powerful as openers. Depending on your audience and the type of written communication you are preparing, here are some things a good ending should do: summarize the main points or your overall thesis, state your conclusions, make recommendations, and relate the ending to the opening.

The type of communication determines the length of an ending. A formal report might have a summary, followed by conclusions, followed by recommendations. A short memo report might have a single-paragraph conclusion tied into the opening remarks. A letter might do no more than ask for some type of reader response in the last paragraph:

Please let me know your decision by Thursday, October 5, 19 __ .

Although the ending that goes on and on, almost like the beginning of a new message, is ineffective, an ending that is too brief is also unsatisfactory in some cases. Take this example from an internal company memo:

> The company, therefore, has no alternative but to close its Atlanta facility.

That may have been a logical conclusion, but what next? The readers surely thought of many questions that were still unanswered: What will happen to the Atlanta employees? Which division will take over the Atlanta activity? How will this affect the company's stability? Endings must provide enough answers, without being long-winded, so readers are not driven to total exasperation. Something like this would have been better:

> The company, therefore, has no alternative but to close its Atlanta facility. We will immediately set up a task force to handle the relocation of employees and the reallocation of resources and activity. With proper management, this difficult decision should eventually improve the company's distribution of assets and strengthen its position in the marketplace.

Both openings and endings tell the reader a lot about the writer's grasp of a subject. The extent to which they unite the different parts of the message and the extent to which they capture the reader's attention and leave the reader with the desired impression say a lot about a writer's skill in communication. Powerful openers and effective endings are primary indicators of an effective business writing style.

Choosing Precise Words

Although business writers must learn to evaluate a message in terms of how it affects their readers, words—individual words and word phrases—mean different things to different people at different times. This elastic or changing nature results because words have both denotations and connotations. *Denotations* are the specific meanings (as found in a dictionary, for example), and *connotations* are the implications apart from specific meanings. Take the following examples. What *precisely* do they mean?

That was a *good* meeting.

This photocopier is a *real bargain*.

The report is *meaningful*.

Each reader may gain a different impression. This problem is inevitable when words are vague or abstract. Some readers may reach the wrong conclusions; others may reach no conclusion at all and will simply wonder, "What does it mean?" This doubt can be easily erased by substituting precise words and meanings:

The meeting resolved two of our three major problems.

This photocopier costs $200 less than other competitive models.

The report provides specific suggestions for improving productivity.

If being precise is that simple, why do so many business people use imprecise and abstract words? Business writing authorities believe that laziness is one reason. It takes less mental effort to say "That was a good meeting" than "The meeting resolved two of our three major problems." Failure to develop a broad vocabulary is another reason. Many of us never try to expand our vocabulary to include the words that identify various shades of meaning. We call everything "good," "meaningful," and so on. Thus John Doe is referred to as a *good* employee rather than a *loyal* employee or a *hardworking* employee or a *cooperative* employee. Also, some business people believe abstract words sound impressive. Everything is an *activity*, a *capacity*, an *operation*, a *system*, a *property*, a *condition*, or something equally vague. Sometimes a writer does not want to divulge the details of a specific system or operation, and some writing intentionally refers to systems or operations in general. In other cases, abstract references are used but are then immediately followed by descriptive details. Business writers have no excuse for using abstract words when specific examples would give readers a better understanding:

Poor: Conditions caused us to halt production in our Omaha plant.

Better: A strike halted production in our Omaha plant.

No matter what the reason is for the use of abstract words, the result is the same in most instances: weak, imprecise business communication.

Can you solve this problem of imprecise writing by increasing your vocabulary or by being less lazy about your business writing? You can in part, but unfortunately another aspect of the problem remains. Personal judgments and prejudice may also affect the preciseness of your writing. (See chapter 4, "Nondiscriminatory Communication.") Look at this statement:

> Jane Smith advocated a liberal position in the debate, and William Brown adopted a conservative stance.

Would Jane Smith and William Brown agree with that analysis? Or would both insist that their views were moderate? Did the writer assign the labels *liberal* and *conservative* out of prejudice? Or were the labels based upon personal judgment rather than identification with a political party? Is that the writer's intent, to reflect a personal bias? The answer is probably sometimes yes and sometimes no. The motive for and intent of a political message are different from the motive for and intent of a scientific report. But in both cases you want your readers to interpret your words a certain way. No matter what personal bias influences your word choice, you don't want your readers to misunderstand your intent.

Sales material readily reveals the weakness of imprecise writing. Which of these messages would most likely lure you into a store?

> *Imprecise:*   Enjoy special savings during our Washington's birthday sale!
>
> *Precise:*   Enjoy savings up to 75% during our Washington's birthday sale!

If the store were offering savings of, say, no more than 5 to 10 percent, it might be better to make the message less specific. But in most other instances, a precise message will outpull an imprecise message. Consider this example from a promotional letter and how it might have been restated to be more precise and thus more effective:

> *Imprecise:*   Each issue of *Product Trends* will increase your knowledge and fatten your pocketbook. If you want to learn more and save more at the same time, subscribe to *Product Trends* today!
>
> *Precise:*   Each issue of *Product Trends* will tell you about new products and recent improvements in old products—practical information that will make

you a wiser shopper and show you how to stretch
your dollars. If you want to buy more but spend
less, subscribe to *Product Trends* today!

The message could be rewritten in several ways depending on what
points you want to stress. But the objective in any case should be to use
more specific words about *what* knowledge is involved (product information) and *how* one can presumably make or save money (shopping
more wisely).

If you need a rule to guide you, keep this thought in mind: Always
use precise words except when you have a special need to be vague or
general. With precise words, your sentences will be stronger, your
messages will be clearer to the reader, and your writing style will be
more effective. You have no doubt noticed that the reader is the key to
everything you do as far as business communications are concerned.
Precise words help readers understand what you mean and visualize
what you are describing. Look at the difference in these examples:

Vague: The report is well organized.

Precise: The report is organized into four sections cover-
             ing each step in the manufacturing process.

The vague statement gives the reader no mental picture of the presentation. In some messages, the reader must have help in forming a
mental image or the message will be useless:

Vague: The new pants have the look that every girl
             wants!

Precise: The new pants have that smart look of today—
             straight legs, slim hips, and splashy new fashion
             colors to add zest to your wardrobe!

Vague messages not only use imprecise words, they often say too little.
Although the importance of conciseness (described earlier in this chapter) cannot be overestimated, messages that lack adequate detail may
be too vague for the reader to absorb and mentally picture the thing
being described. The above example—"The new pants have the look
that every girl wants!"—is a case of using imprecise words and saying
too little.

Vague words may say little about the subject, but they tell a great
deal about the writer. Imprecise language is often the telltale sign of
someone who doesn't have a firm grasp of the subject. Readers might

easily conclude that the writer in the first example below hasn't done enough homework:

Imprecise: Work on our upcoming conference program is progressing nicely. Committees have activity in motion, and registration is accelerating. Prospective speakers are beginning to respond to invitations to present papers.

Precise: The program for our annual conference is three-fourths complete; twelve session topics must be selected for parallel sessions on Friday, March 5. The facilities committee reports that room reservations will be confirmed by the hotel today. The equipment and transportation committees have received their assignments and will submit progress reports on February 1. Eighty-four registration forms have arrived; over half of them in the past two days. Finally, about half of the invited speakers have accepted our invitation to present papers; the rest have been asked to reply by the end of this week.

How much detail you use depends upon your reader. A conference chairman would want more facts and figures than a curious business associate. The conference chairman, for instance, would be interested in knowing that twelve session topics still had to be selected for Friday's parallel sessions. But a curious business associate would be satisfied to learn that the program is three-fourths complete. Even a curious business associate would be unimpressed with no more than a glib remark that the program is progressing nicely.

Some business people mistakenly assume that the most complex word is the most precise word. Often the opposite is true. The preciseness of a word is never measured by the number of letters it contains. Look at this sentence taken from a company memo about finding a better way to take inventory each year:

The conclusion developed upon investigation of the potential implications accentuated the requirements for positive action.

No one (probably including the writer) will ever know exactly what that means. In simple language it may mean:

Because of previous problems, we need to develop a better sytem for taking inventory.

Then again, you may decide the writer meant something else, and that's the point: Complex words contribute nothing to precise communication. They often serve to befuddle a message and confuse the reader. Why do some writers say *deprivation* when they mean *loss?* Why do they say *recondite* when they mean *hidden* or *concealed?* Even when the words are familiar and the message is obvious, a simple statement will nevertheless be more clear and precise to most readers:

> *Complex:* Excessive temperatures caused the destructive scaling and stripping of the paint.
>
> *Simple:* Extreme heat made the paint peel.

Perhaps the writer felt a need to make the statement sound more important in the above example. Making simple things sound complex is a favorite tactic of some business people. But it seldom works. Writers only make fools of themselves when they treat something such as peeling paint as if it were a devastation created by a nuclear holocaust. Precise, simple language—not abstract, complex language—is the mark of better business writing.

Avoiding Cold and Pompous Writing

Cold and pompous writing affects readers in several ways. Some readers shake their heads in disbelief to think that a writer could be such a stuffed shirt; others bristle because the writer sounds like an unfriendly, uncaring snob; some wonder if anything worth comprehending is hidden behind the cumbersome parade of cold and pompous words and expressions. This type of writing is offensive to almost everyone, including other pompous writers. Yet many business people persistently cling to their cold and pompous writing style, unaware that they are creating a counterproductive, negative image of themselves and the organizations they represent.

Business people mistakenly believe that only one alternative—a chatty, frivolous approach—exists for the cold and pompous treatment. Not so! Dignified, formal, and objective material can be concise, simple, clear, and precise without going to either extreme. But if a cold and pompous style has become a habit, it may take some serious work for you to develop a more pleasing and successful style. The first step is to recognize that vogue words, jargon, euphemisms, unnecessary prefixes and suffixes, and roundabout gobbledygook are all signs of a weak and ineffective style. Consider this paragraph from an informal business report:

> The employer owes certain duties of protection to the employees. If he neglects to use due care in the performance of these duties, he is liable for the injurious consequences of his neglect.

The above paragraph is a boring and pretentious way of stating a simple fact:

> Employers must protect their employees in certain ways. If they don't, they are liable for any injuries caused by their neglect.

Or take this comment from an attorney's letter to a client:

> Delivery of the instrument is indispensable to the acquisition of legal title to the instrument.

How many lay persons will understand that remark? Some may decide the statement means:

> The instrument has to be delivered to you before you can have legal title to it.

Other readers may read it as:

> You have to deliver the instrument before legal title can pass to the other party.

Someone else may have another interpretation. Such stiff, awkward, pretentious messages leave readers floundering. Effective business messages never leave doubt in a reader's mind. Readers are not impressed with a writer's pomposity; they are disgusted that the writer doesn't use plain, understandable English.

Pompous words are easy to spot. Often they are a long or complex substitute for a short, simple word:

abate, abatement (cut down, decrease, drop)

aggregation (total)

approximately (about)

assistance (aid, help)

behest (request)

bona fide (genuine)

chef d'oeuvre (masterpiece)

cognizant (aware)

commence, inaugurate, initiate (begin, start)

commendation (praise)

commercialization (commerce)

construct (make)

customary channels (usual way)

delineate (describe, draw)

disseminate, promulgate (circulate, send out)

domicile (home)

effected, effectuated (make, did)

endeavoring (trying)

equivalent (equal)

facilitate (ease, help)

forward, transmit (send)

functionalization (use)

germane (relevant)

hiatus (gap, interval)

impair (damage, hurt, weaken)

in toto (altogether)

instantaneously (now, quickly)

instrumentalities (means, ways)

involving, concerning (about)

ipso facto (by the very nature of the case)

lethal (deadly, fatal)

milieu (surroundings, environment)

modus operandi (method)

multitudinous (many)

nadir (low point)

obfuscate (confuse)

obviate (prevent, do away with)

palpable (clear, obvious, visible)

per annum (a year, each year)

per diem (a day, each day)

per se (as such)

peruse (read)

procedural practices (what to do and how to do it)

raison d'etre (reason for)

remuneration (pay)

salient (important)

sine qua non (essential)

succumbed (died)

terminate (end)

utilize, utilization (use)

vicissitude (change)

wherewithal (means)

The main problem with such pompous words is that writers overuse them. But specialized interest groups do have their own specialized vocabularies, and what may sound pompous to one reader may be common language to another. *Palpable* is more common to the medical field than *obvious*, and *ipso facto* is more common to the legal profession than *by the very nature of the case.* Your word choice and writing style depend on your audience.

Vogue words are a special category of pretentious language:

charisma	input
communications	interface
dialogue	mode
dichotomy	super
environment	variable
expertise	viable
feedback	

No one objects to a data processing manager using the term *feed-*

back when describing a new computer terminal. But when the manager goes home and asks his or her son what feedback he got from his science teacher that day, something is wrong. It is one thing for a writer to discuss *communication* in a book about business writing, such as this one, but it is another thing to ask your mother if she received your latest communication. Some people use vogue words and technical language so frequently that their business messages are almost comic:

> I think the program is viable, but I will know more after I interface with Joe and evaluate his input. Another variable to consider is how to phase out the environmental factor. How to implement this activity will affect our mode of operations saleswise, according to a recent dialogue I had with Ellen. And this is another can of worms to contemplate. Her expertise, by the way, has had a super impact on our procedural practices in my judgment. Her charisma will no doubt obviate any dichotomy that tends to sabotage optimum interpersonal relations.

The above paragraph is an example of vogue words, jargon, and gobbledygook all blended together. *Jargon* is the technical slang of a particular interest group. *Gobbledygook* is a tangle of jargon and other vague, abstract words that make a message largely, or at least partially, unintelligible.

Another sign of a cold and pompous business writing style is the *euphemism*. This is an inoffensive substitute for a potentially offensive expression. Thus you read about someone who *passed away*, not died, and a man who is a *maintenance engineer*, not a janitor. Euphemisms have their place and are often preferred to avoid unnecessary bluntness or distasteful references. But it is pretentious to call used furniture *preowned furniture* or to call a traffic light an *electronic visual signal*. The latter example is not only pompous, it is confusing. How many people would know what the writer meant by "electronic visual signal"?

Unnecessary prefixes and suffixes increase the chances of sounding cold and pompous. Notice the difference in tone in these examples:

Poor:	She stopped to give assist*ance* to the stranded motorist.
Better:	She stopped to help the stranded motorist.
Poor:	I am in agree*ment* with your recommendation.

Better:	I agree with your recommendation.
Poor:	She is *hyper*critical of other employees.
Better:	She is excessively critical of other employess.

Although unnecessary use of suffixes and prefixes often makes writing sound stuffy, our language would be weak without these helpers. The trick is to know when you don't need them and to avoid overusing them. For instance, your language sounds more conversational and relaxed when you say "after accepting the award" rather than "after acceptance of the award" or when you write "after determining the cause" rather than "after a determination of the cause."

Business people can greatly improve their writing style by rereading their messages to look for vogue words, jargon, gobbledygook, euphemisms, and unnecessary prefixes and suffixes. All of these things can make your writing sound cold and pompous. Trite expressions (described in the next section) are also stale and wordy obstacles to a natural, pleasing style. An affected style usually makes readers work harder, and it can easily make writers sound as if they have an absurdly inflated sense of self-importance. Using a cold and pompous style is a good way to make a fool of yourself.

The same rule applies over and over whenever you consider good and bad writing habits: *Always* write to help your reader easily and quickly comprehend what you are saying; *never* write to show off to your reader or to make small words and ideas sound more important. Observing this commonsense rule strictly is the easiest way to avoid a cold and pompous business writing style.

Guarding Against Trite Expressions

Most business people use trite expressions unintentionally, out of habit. But some people use them intentionally in an effort to sound businesslike and formal, and that's even worse. Trite expressions are stale, wordy, and stilted. It is amazing how many of these banal words and phrases have found their way into our written and spoken language. Business writers should be on guard for worn-out expressions such as these:

acknowledge receipt of (received)

Trite:	This will acknowledge receipt of your booklet.
Better:	We received your booklet.

advise (say, tell)

> *Trite:* I would like to advise you about a change in our policy.

> *Better:* I would like to tell you about a change in our policy.

after giving due consideration (after considering)

> *Trite:* After giving due considerations to the proposal, we decided to request other recommendations.

> *Better:* After considering the proposal, we decided to request other recommendations.

allow me to express our appreciation (thank you for, we appreciate)

> *Trite:* Allow me to express our appreciation for your offer to help.

> *Better:* We appreciate your offer to help.

along these lines (be specific)

> *Trite:* I plan to discuss progress along these lines.

> *Better:* I plan to discuss progress in air pollution control.

and oblige (delete)

> *Trite:* Kindly send the following items and oblige.

> *Better:* Please send the following items immediately.

as per (according to)

> *Trite:* The material has been assembled as per your instructions.

> *Better:* The material has been assembled according to your instructions.

as soon as possible (be specific)

> *Trite:* Please reply as soon as possible.

> *Better:* Please reply by Friday, June 4, 19____.

at all times (always)

> *Trite:*   We are happy to hear from you at all times.
>
> *Better:*   We are always happy to hear from you.

at an early date, at your convenience *(give a specific date)*

> *Trite:*   Please return the enclosed filmstrip at an early date.
>
> *Better:*   Please return the enclosed filmstrip by Wednesday, March 27, 19____.

at this time (now)

> *Trite:*   We are ready to start production at this time.
>
> *Better:*   We are ready to start production now.

at hand *(delete)*

> *Trite:*   I have your report at hand.
>
> *Better:*   I have your report.

attached please find, enclosed please find (attached, enclosed)

> *Trite:*   Enclosed please find an itinerary and flight schedule.
>
> *Better:*   Enclosed are an itinerary and flight schedule.

at the present writing, at this time (now)

> *Trite:*   Sales are up at the present writing.
>
> *Better:*   Sales are up now.

awaiting your favor (I hope to hear from you soon)

> *Trite:*   Awaiting your favor, I remain. . . .
>
> *Better:*   I hope to hear from you soon.

beg *(delete)*

> *Trite:* I beg to inform you that the East Coast branch has started its new time-sharing program.

> *Better:* The East Coast branch has started its new time-sharing program.

contents carefully noted *(delete)*

> *Trite:* Yours of the 20th received and contents carefully noted.

> *Better:* The list of prospective customers in your April 20 letter has been sent to our sales manager.

duly *(delete)*

> *Trite:* Your order has been duly forwarded to our shipping department.

> *Better:* We have sent your order to our shipping department.

enclosed please find (enclosed)

> *Trite:* Enclosed please find our check for $33.27.

> *Better:* Enclosed is our check for $33.27.

esteemed *(delete)*

> *Trite:* We received your esteemed favor of the 3rd.

> *Better:* Thank you for your letter of October 3.

favor *(do not use for check, letter, or order; be specific)*

> *Trite:* We appreciated your favor of January 7.

> *Better:* We appreciated your order of January 7.

for your careful consideration *(delete)*

> *Trite:* I am enclosing a report on trends in terracing for your careful consideration.

> *Better:*   I am enclosing a report on trends in terracing.

for your information *(delete)*

> *Trite:*   A revised prospectus is enclosed for your informa-
>   tion.
>
> *Better:*   A revised prospectus is enclosed.

hand you (enclosed is)

> *Trite:*   We herewith hand you our remittance of $89.60.
>
> *Better:*   Enclosed is our check for $89.60.

have before me (in answer, in reply, thank you for)

> *Trite:*   I have before me a copy of your August 5, 19____,
>   Executive Bulletin.
>
> *Better:*   Thank you for the copy of your August 5, 19____,
>   Executive Bulletin.

hereto *(delete)*

> *Trite:*   I am attaching hereto a sketch of the new nurs-
>   ing home.
>
> *Better:*   Here is a sketch of the new nursing home.

herewith *(delete)*

> *Trite:*   Enclosed herewith is a sample purchase and sale
>   agreement.
>
> *Better:*   Enclosed is a sample purchase and sale agree-
>   ment.

in re (regarding, concerning)

> *Trite:*   This is information in re the Parker resolution.
>
> *Better:*   This is information regarding the Parker resolu-
>   tion.

in receipt of (we received, thank you for)

> *Trite:*   We are in receipt of the new engineering guide-
> lines.
>
> *Better:*   Thank you for the new engineering guidelines.

in the amount of (for)

> *Trite:*   Enclosed is our check in the amount of $17.20.
>
> *Better:*   Enclosed is our check for $17.20.

in the event that (if, in case)

> *Trite:*   We will break for coffee in the event that the
> meeting runs late.
>
> *Better:*   We will break for coffee if the meeting runs late.

line (merchandise, line of goods)

> *Trite:*   We will introduce our new line on Thursday.
>
> *Better:*   We will introduce our new merchandise on
> Thursday.

our Mr. Daniels (Mr. Daniels)

> *Trite:*   Our Mr. Daniels will telephone you.
>
> *Better:*   Mr. Daniels will telephone you.

per day (a day)

> *Trite:*   The cabin is forty dollars per day.
>
> *Better:*   The cabin is forty dollars a day.

permit me to say (*delete*)

> *Trite:*   Permit me to say that your fall catalog will appeal
> to shoppers of all ages.
>
> *Better:*   Your fall catalog will appeal to shoppers of all
> ages.

please be advised that *(delete)*

> *Trite:*   Please be advised that the merger will be an-
>   nounced at the press conference on Monday, De-
>   cember 7, 19____.
>
> *Better:*   The merger will be announced at the press con-
>   ference on Monday, December 7, 19____.

recent date *(be specific)*

> *Trite:*   I received your memo of recent date.
>
> *Better:*   I received your memo of February 16, 19____.

replying to yours of (thank you for)

> *Trite:*   This is replying to yours of the 9th.
>
> *Better:*   Thank you for your letter of May 9.

same (it, they, them)

> *Trite:*   Your 5,000 letterheads are being printed now. We
>   will ship same on the 12th.
>
> *Better:*   Your 5,000 letterheads are being printed now,
>   and we will ship them on Tuesday, August 12,
>   19____.

state (say, tell)

> *Trite:*   I'll state my plan later.
>
> *Better:*   I'll tell you my plan later.

take pleasure (are pleased, are happy, are glad)

> *Trite:*   We take pleasure in announcing the appointment
>   of Donald Harris as district supervisor.
>
> *Better:*   We are happy to announce the appointment of
>   Donald Harris as district supervisor.

thanking you in advance (I would appreciate)

> *Trite:*   Thanking you in advance for any information you
>   may have.
>
> *Better:*   I would appreciate any information you may
>   have.

thank you kindly (thank you)

> *Trite:*   Thank you kindly for your suggestions.
>
> *Better:*   Thank you for your suggestions.

the undersigned (I)

> *Trite:*   The undersigned will appreciate any help you
>   can provide.
>
> *Better:*   I will appreciate any help you can provide.

the writer (I)

> *Trite:*   The writer has had several similar experiences.
>
> *Better:*   I have had several similar experiences.

this letter is for the purpose of *(delete)*

> *Trite:*   This letter is for the purpose of introducing our
>   new desk-top minicomputer for small businesses.
>   This computer is compact and easy to use.
>
> *Better:*   Our new desk-top minicomputer for small busi-
>   nesses is compact and easy to use.

this will acknowledge receipt of (thank you for)

> *Trite:*   This will acknowledge receipt of your registra-
>   tion.
>
> *Better:*   Thank you for your registration.

too numerous to mention (numerous, many)

> *Trite:*   The reasons for their failure are too numerous to
>   mention.

Better: The reasons for their failure are numerous.

under separate cover *(be specific)*

Trite: The blueprints were sent under separate cover.

Better: The blueprints were sent by registered first-class mail.

up to this writing (until now)

Trite: Orders have been heavy up to this writing.

Better: Orders have been heavy until now.

valued *(delete)*

Trite: We appreciate your valued order.

Better: We appreciate your order.

we regret to inform you (we are sorry)

Trite: We regret to inform you that your photographs arrived damaged.

Better: We are sorry that your photographs arrived damaged.

wish to say, wish to state, would say *(delete)*

Trite: We wish to state that the company has no plans to relocate.

Better: The company has no plans to relocate.

you claim, you say, you state *(delete)*

Trite: You claim that your check was sent three weeks ago.

Better: We are sorry that the check you sent three weeks ago never arrived.

yours of *(be specific)*

>   *Trite:*   Thank you for yours of recent date.
>
>   *Better:*   Thank you for your order of September 13,
>   19___.

You often see trite expressions such as *acknowledge receipt of* and *enclosed please find* in business letters and memos. Other business communications also have their share of trite expressions such as *in the event that* and *up to this writing*. It often seems that business people work at being dull and wordy. Think how often you read *prior to* instead of *before, on the grounds that* instead of *because, subsequent to* instead of *after,* and *with regard to* instead of *about.*

The problem is not so much that business writers make occasional slips, but that they continually and often deliberately overload their business messages with imprecise, unnecessary, pompous, trite expressions, all of which obscure meanings, weaken messages, and frustrate readers. Ineffective communication creates problems; effective communication solves problems. Often it takes a lot of discipline and practice to develop a strong, productive style. But it is worth the effort, because success in the working world depends heavily on your ability to write clearly and effectively.

2 GUIDE TO CORRECT WORD USE

Choosing the correct word should be no problem for a business person, right? Wrong. It is such a serious problem that many authorities have compiled lists, even complete books, of troublesome words and phrases. This chapter is a guide to words and expressions that are commonly misused in business writing. You will notice that some of these words and expressions may have additional meanings not described here; this list primarily consists of selected examples of common misuse. In reading the definitions, you may discover that authorities do not always agree on matters of word usage. Your best guide in such instances is to *be consistent* no matter what usage you adopt. (Consult any modern dictionary for problems involving meaning, spelling, pronunciation, and word division.)

a while/awhile

A while, a noun phrase, refers to a period or interval. (If you can wait a while longer, the copier will be fixed by noon.)

Awhile, an adverb, means "for a short period or interval." (The manager wanted to work awhile before leaving the office.) Do not use *for* with *awhile* (*not* for awhile) since *for* is implied.

ability/capacity

Ability means "the physical or mental power to do something." (He has the ability to solve complex equations.)

Capacity means "a physical measure of content" (capacity of two tons) or "the power to absorb or learn something." (His capacity for science is limited.)

about/around/round

About means several things: "in the area" (about here), "nearly or approximately" (about five years), "almost" (about finished). Do not use *at* with *about* (*not* at about five years). Also, do not use *about* unnecessarily (*not* about fifty to sixty years old).

Around is often used in place of *about* (stop around noon), although authorities discourage this habit. It is used informally to describe "here and there" (drive around, wait around).

Round is a colloquial substitute for *about*. (I'll see you round eight o'clock.)

abridged/unabridged

Abridged means "reduced; shortened" (an abridged version of the report).

Unabridged means the opposite of *abridged*: "not reduced or shortened; complete" (the unabridged, original document).

accept/except

Accept means "to receive, to take; to agree with, to say yes." (I accept your offer.)

Except, as a verb, means "to make an exception of; to omit or exclude." (He was excepted from the list of prospective speakers.) As a preposition, it means "other than." (Everyone agreed except Lois.)

accidentally/accidently

Accidentally means "by chance; without design." (He hit the post accidentally.)

Accidently is a mispronounced and misspelled version of *accidentally*.

acknowledge/admit

Acknowledge means "to concede; to grant; to say that something is true." (The manager acknowledged the problem.)

Admit also means "to concede or to say that something is true" (she admitted her mistake) but is used more often to suggest the involvement of force or pressure.

adapt/adept/adopt

Adapt means "to change something for one's own purpose; to adjust." (I adapted the meter to our console.)

Adept means "proficient, skilled." (She is adept in foreign languages.)

Adopt means "to accept something without changing it." (They adopted the resolutions.)

adverse/averse
Adverse means "opposed; strongly disinclined." (The company had an adverse reaction to the union's action.)

Averse means "reluctant; having a distaste for." (She is averse to romantic involvements at work.)

advice/advise
Advice, a noun, means "a recommendation or suggestion." (My advice is to place your order before the holiday rush.)

Advise, a verb, means "to counsel, to give advice." (The president advises all employees to observe the new safety regulations.) *Advise* is often misused in business correspondence for *tell* or *say*.

affect/effect
Affect, a verb, means "to influence." (How will this policy affect our schedule?)

Effect, as a noun, means "a result." (What effect did the speech have on the audience?) As a verb, it means "to bring about." (The new policy will effect better customer relations.)

afflict/inflict
Afflict means "to distress; to trouble; to injure." (Alcoholism afflicts many executives in stressful positions.)

Inflict means "to impose; to cause to be endured." (He inflicted his tyrannical attitude on the already overworked staff.)

aid/assist/help
Aid means "to provide relief or assistance" and suggests incapacity or helplessness on the part of the recipient. (The government provided aid to flood victims.)

Assist means "to support or aid" and suggests a secondary role. (Her staff will assist in the presentation.)

Help means "to assist; to promote; to relieve; to benefit" and suggests steps toward some end. (He helped them move the machine.)

aim/intend

Aim refers to a matter of positioning (take aim) or means "to try." (I aim to meet our goal.)

Intend means "to plan on; to design." (The task force intends to complete its work this week.)

all ready/already

All ready, an adjective, means "completely ready." (The presentation will begin when they are all ready.)

Already, an adverb, means "previously." (The plant was already closed when we arrived.)

all right/alright

All right means "safe; acceptable; yes." (The schematic looks all right to me.)

Alright is a misspelling of *all right*.

all together/altogether

All together refers to everyone in the same place. (The staff was all together for the Christmas party.)

Altogether means "wholly; completely; all told." (Altogether, we accomplished a great deal.) *Completely* is preferred by some authorities in reference to *wholly*.

alter/change

Alter means "to make different without changing into something else." (She altered the curtains befor hanging them.)

Change also means "to make different" but is not restricted in the sense that *alter* is. (He changed into a tuxedo for dinner.)

although/though

Although means "regardless; even though." It is preferred over *though* at the beginning of a sentence. (Although the plan failed, we learned a lot from the experience.)

Though means the same thing but is used more to link words and phrases in the middle of a sentence. (It is true though that the index is too high.)

amend/emend
> *Amend* means "to improve; to make right." (The directors want to amend the bylaws.)
>
> *Emend* means "to correct; to alter." (The editor will no doubt emend the introduction.)

among/between
> *Among* refers to the relationship of more than two things. (The exchange of opinions among the participants was hostile.)
>
> *Between* refers to the relationship of two things or more than two things if each one is individually related to the others. (The exchange of opinions between Smith and Wright was hostile).

anxious/eager
> *Anxious* refers to uneasiness or worry. (I am anxious to know the outcome of the surgery.)
>
> *Eager* sugests earnest desire or anticipation. (I am eager to start my new job.)

anybody/anyone
> *Anybody* means "one person" and takes a singular verb. It is spelled as two words in reference to an actual body. (The police could not find any body in the room.)
>
> *Anyone* means the same thing as *anybody*. (Anyone is welcome.) Authorities frequently recommend using *anyone* instead of *anybody*.

appraise/apprise
> *Appraise* means "to estimate." (He appraised the property and recommended a sales price.)
>
> *Apprise* means "to inform." (We apprised him of our progress.)

apt/liable/likely
> *Apt* means "fit" (apt in journalism) or "inclined to do something" (apt to come early).
>
> *Liable* means "obligated by law; responsible." (The company is liable if an accident occurs on the property.)
>
> *Likely* means "probable." (An economic slowdown is likely.)

as/since

As is a less effective conjunction than *since*, but it has other uses in the English language: preposition, adverb, and pronoun.

Since (or *because*, *when*) is more effective and is preferred. (Since this issue is late, we will have to reschedule the next issue.)

as . . . as/so . . . as

As . . . as is preferred for positive expressions. (The next conference will be as successful as the last one.)

So . . . as is often preferred, but not essential, for negative expressions. (The revised proposal is not so good as the original version.)

as if/as though/like

As if is less formal than *as though*. (She hesitated to begin the project as if she were afraid it would fail.)

As though is used in the same sense, and like *as if*, it is followed by a verb in the subjunctive mood. (He angrily rejected the proposal as though it were a personal affront.)

Like is widely used and misused in informal conversation (like I said), but authorities still recommend that it be used as a preposition and with a noun or pronoun that is *not* followed by a verb. (The president acts like a dictator.)

assure/ensure/insure

Assure means "to guarantee." It is used only in reference to persons. (I can assure you that we intend to complete the job on schedule.)

Ensure, a less common variation of *insure*, means "to make certain." (This long-range policy will ensure our continuing success.)

Insure, the preferred spelling of ensure, also means "to make certain; to guard against risk or loss." (The mail room will insure the package.)

balance/remainder

Balance refers to "a degree of equality" (we want to balance the budget) or to "bookkeeping" (please double-check the balance in our account).

Remainder should be used in all other instances to mean "what is left over." (Five hundred of the 1,000 brochures were mailed this morning, and the remainder are almost ready for mailing now.)

barely/hardly/scarcely

Barely means "meagerly; narrowly." (He could barely fit into the small foreign car.)

Hardly means "with difficulty." (She could hardly control the car in the driving rain.)

Scarcely means "by a narrow margin" and suggests something hard to believe. (He could scarcely believe his application was rejected.)

Do not use a negative with any of these terms since each already has a negative quality (*not* not barely, not hardly, or not scarcely).

because/due to

Because should be used with nonlinking verbs. (They were exhausted because of overwork.)

Due to means "caused by" and is followed by a linking verb. (Their exhaustion was due to overwork.) *Due to* is often used by careless business writers as a wordy substitute for *since* or *because*.

begin/commence

Begin means "to start; to cause something to come into being." (Let's begin.)

Commence means the same thing but should be reserved for legal or other formal writing. *Begin* is preferred in most business communications.

beside/besides

Beside, a preposition, means "next to." (He parked the van beside the shipping entrance.)

Besides, most commonly used as an adverb, means "in addition to" (we have another report besides this one to get out) or "moreover." (Besides, I have more pressing matters to handle.)

bilateral/unilateral

Bilateral means "affecting two sides." (The bilateral treaty imposed stiff conditions on both countries.)

Unilateral means "affecting one side; undertaken by one party." (The president's unilateral decision met strong resistance.)

brochure/leaflet/pamphlet

Brochure refers to a small booklet or pamphlet.

Leaflet refers to a folded or unfolded, single printed sheet, not stitched or trimmed at the fold.

Pamphlet refers to an unbound, printed publication with a paper cover or no cover.

The three terms are often used loosely and interchangeably in the business world, without agreement on exact meanings.

can/may

Can refers to ability. (He can sell anything.)

May refers to permission. (You may begin negotiations any time.)

candid/frank

Candid means "open; straightforward." (Her remarks were candid.)

Frank means the same thing but suggests an outspoken, possibly less tactful remark. (The two opponents had a frank exchange of views.)

canvas/canvass

Canvas, a noun, means "a closely woven cloth." (The oil painting was done on canvas.)

Canvass, a verb, means 'to solicit votes or opinions." ((The magazine wanted to canvass the neighborhood.)

capital/capitol

Capital means "a stock or value of goods." (The company needed more capital to expand.) It also means "the city that is the seat of government." (Concord is the capital of New Hampshire.)

Capitol refers to a state building. It is always capitalized in reference to the seat of the United States Congress. (The Capitol in Washington, D.C., is a magnificient structure.)

censor/censure

Censor means "to examine for possible deletions." (The editor censors all manuscripts.)

Censure means "to condemn; to blame." (The committee censured the derogatory report.)

client/customer/patron

Client refers to someone who consults a professional person." (The attorney met his client at the airport.)

Customer refers to someone who purchases a commodity or service. (The salesperson helped the customer make a selection.)

Patron has the same meaning as *customer* but also refers to someone who supports someone or something. (The chairman of the board was well known in the East as a patron of the arts.)

close/near

Close means "very near" (close race) or "intimate" (close friend).

Near means "closely related" (near neighbors) or "narrow margin" (a near victory).

close/shut

Close means "to prevent passage to or from." (Close the door.)

Shut, which has the same meaning as *close*, is more emphatic. It also means "to suspend operations." (They shut down the generator.)

common/mutual

Common refers to the sharing of something. (They have a common purpose.)

Mutual refers to something directed by one or more persons to one or more other persons. (The two competitors had a mutual respect for each other.)

comparatively/relatively

Comparatively refers to a degree of comparison (the winter was comparatively mild), but is often misused when no comparison with another factor is intended.

Relatively refers to the state of something in relation to something else. (The drug is relatively fast acting.) *Relatively* is used improperly and unnecessarily by many business writers.

compare/contrast

Compare means "to examine for difference or similarity, mostly similarity." *Compare* is followed by *with* when specifics are examined. (She compared her record with his.) But in a general reference, *compare* is followed by *to*. (Compared to yesterday, today is tranquil.)

Contrast means "to show only differences." The noun form of *contrast* is followed by *to*. (The new typewriters have correcting features in contrast to the old models.) But the verb *contrast* is usually followed by *with*. (His present position contrasts markedly with his old one.)

complement/compliment

Complement means "to complete." (The new study complements the previous report.)

Compliment means "to flatter or praise." (His employer complimented him on his achievement.)

complementary/supplementary

Complementary means "completing to make up the whole." (The printing and binding operations are complementary.)

Supplementary means "added to something." (The catastrophy insurance is supplementary to his basic policy.)

compose/comprise

Compose means "to make up by combining." (Seven rooms compose the suite. *or* The suite is composed of seven rooms.) A general rule is that the parts (seven rooms) compose the whole (the suite.)

Comprise means "to include." (The company comprises two hundred employees.) A general rule is that the whole (the company) comprises the parts (the employees).

concept/idea/notion

Concept refers to something complete or generalized. (He formulated his concept of retrogression.)

Idea refers to a plan, a thought, or a representation. (This is not my idea of a smooth operation).

Notion suggests an inconclusive or vague thought. (She had no notion that the restaurant would be closed.)

connotation/denotation

Connotation is the suggested meaning of words beyond the dictionary definition. For example, *shrewdness* implies dishonesty to some people.

Denotation is the primary dictionary meaning of words. For example, *shrewd* is defined in the dictionary as "clever, discerning awareness."

consistently/constantly

Consistently means "with uniformity or regularity; steady continuity." (He consistently pursued the same theme in all of his speeches.)

Constantly means "with steadfast resolution; faithfulness" (they have been a constant ally) or "without interruption" (the machines ran constantly).

continual/continuous

Continual means "always going on; repeated over and over," and often implies a steady or rapid succession. (The company is continually seeking part-time help.)

Continuous means "connected; unbroken; going on without interruption." (The computer is in continuous operation, day and night.)

continue/resume

Continue means "to keep on without interruption." (She continued working through the night.)

Resume means "to start again after interruptions." (They resumed operations after the equipment was repaired.)

convince/persuade
    Convince means "to lead someone to understand, agree, or be-
    lieve." (She convinced her employer that funding was inade-
    quate.)

    Persuade means "to win someone over." (I persuaded him to
    take the day off.)

covert/overt
    Covert means "hidden." (The agency was conducting covert
    operations.)

    Overt means "open to view." (The staff's political work was
    always overt.)

credible/creditable
    Credible means "believable; reasonable." (His reason for fail-
    ing to appear is credible.)

    Creditable means "deserving credit; worthy of praise." (Her
    speech was creditable.)

currently/presently
    Currently means "the time now passing; belonging to the
    present time." (The company is currently being formed.)

    Presently means "shortly or before long." (She will arrive pres-
    ently.)

customary/usual
    Customary means "according to usual practices." (It is cus-
    tomary in this office to stagger the lunch breaks.)

    Usual means "something common, normal, or ordinary." (He
    left for work at the usual time.)

decisive/incisive
    Decisive means "conclusive; final." (The election was a deci-
    sive victory for the Republicans.)

    Incisive means "direct; cutting; clear-cut." (His decisions are
    always incisive.)

deduction/induction
    Deduction refers to reasoning by moving from the general to
    the particular. (All computers accept some form of symbolic
    data; therefore, the XL100 should accept this symbolic input.)

Induction refers to reasoning by moving from the particular to the general. (Having read thousands of business letters, most of which have one or more grammatical errors, I believe that most business people need further education in basic English composition.)

defer/delay/postpone

Defer means "to put off something until later." (He deferred his decision until next week.)

Delay means "to set aside; to detain; to stop." (Let's delay further work on that project.)

Postpone means "to put off something until later, with full intention of undertaking it at a specific time." (The director postponed the meeting until Wednesday, October 6.)

degree/extent

Degree refers to a step or stage. (He went along with the proposal to a degree.) Both *degree* and *extent* are overused in business writing: "to the extent that," "to the degree that," "to some extent/degree."

Extent refers to the range or scope of something. (The extent of his authority was sharply curtailed by the governing board.)

deny/refute

Deny means "to disclaim; to refuse." (He denied ever seeing the witness at the site.)

Refute means "to prove wrong." (She cleverly refuted the plaintiff's contention.)

depositary/depository

Depositary means "a person or group entrusted with something." (The trustees of the gallery are the depositaries.)

Depository means "a place used for safekeeping something." (The bank vault will serve as a depository for the documents.)

different from/different than/different to

Different from, is preferred by careful business writers. (My objective is different from yours.)

Different than is sometimes used when followed by a clause.

(The results were different than he had expected they would be.)

Different to is a form of British usage.

differentiate/distinguish
> *Differentiate* means "to show in detail a difference in." (You can differentiate among the paper samples by weight and grain.)
>
> *Distinguish* also means "to show the difference in" but is used to point out general differences that separate one category from another. (You can easily distinguish radios from television sets.)

disability/inability
> *Disability* suggests a mental or physical impairment. (The applicant was hired in spite of his physical disability.)
>
> *Inability* suggests a lack of power or capacity. (She failed the entrance exam because of her inability to handle complex scientific data.)

disinterested/uninterested
> *Disinterested* means "objective, free from selfish motive; unbiased." (The researchers remained disinterested while making their survey.)
>
> *Uninterested* means "indifferent, not interested." (He was uninterested in the new office decor.)

disorganized/unorganized
> *Disorganized* means "lack of an orderly system; lack of coherence." (A disorganized person would never succeed in this position.)
>
> *Unorganized* means "not characterized by an orderly whole." (The disgruntled workers were unorganized.)

displace/misplace
> *Displace* means "to move something from its usual place." (A collision displaced the sign at the entrance.)
>
> *Misplace* means "to put in a wrong place." (I misplaced the Henderson file.)

disqualified/unqualified
> *Disqualified* means "made ineligible; deprived of." (He was disqualified from entering the academy.)

> *Unqualified* means "not having the required qualifications; not fit." (She was unqualified for the position.)

disregardless/irregardless
> *Disregardless* is used improperly for *regardless*.

> *Irregardless* is also used improperly for *regardless*. In both cases, the prefixes *dis-* and *ir-* are unnecessary. (Regardless of the outcome, I am going ahead with our plan.)

dissatisfied/unsatisfied
> *Dissatisfied* means "unhappy; upset; displeased." (She is dissatisfied with her new position.)

> *Unsatisfied* means "not content, not pleased; wanting something more or better to be done." (The supervisor was unsatisfied with the quality of the work.)

doubt if/doubt that/doubt whether
> *Doubt if* should be avoided in business writing.

> *Doubt that* is the preferred expression in negative or interrogative sentences when little doubt exists. (I doubt that we can meet the deadline.)

> *Doubt whether* is usually limited to situations involving strong uncertainty. (I doubt whether anything will come of it.)

each other/one another
> *Each other* is used when referring to two persons or objects. (The two attorneys consulted each other before taking action.)

> *One another* is used when referring to three or more persons or objects. (The six candidates were debating with one another off camera as well as on camera.)

effective/effectual/efficient
> *Effective* means "producing the desired result" and applies to either agents or their action. The emphasis is on the production of the desired effect. (The publicity was effective.)

> *Effectual* means "able to produce a desired result" and usually applies to the action. The emphasis is on the thing that was

able to produce the desired effect. (Her efforts were effectual in gaining the necessary support.)

Efficient means "capable of producing the desired result" and applies to agents, their action, or the instrument used. The emphasis is on the capability of producing the desired effect. (They run an efficient organization.)

elicit/illicit/licit

Elicit means "to bring out." (The questionnaire attempted to elicit a favorable response.)

Illicit means "unlawful." (The store was a front for illicit drug traffic.)

Licit means "permissible." (The promoter engaged in strictly licit activities.)

emigrate/immigrate

Emigrate means "to move from one place to another." (Feldman emigrated from Israel last year.)

Immigrate means "to enter a country to establish permanent residence." (O'Connell immigrated to the United States this spring.)

eminent/imminent

Eminent means "distinguished; conspicuous" (the eminent scholar).

Imminent means "impending" (an imminent disaster).

endless/ innumerable

Endless means "boundless; interminable." (The sky is endless.)

Innumerable means "countless; too many to count." (The duties of a secretary are innumerable.)

envisage/envision

Envisage means "to confront; to plan; to view in a particular way." (I envisage a four-story structure with one executive dining room and two employee cafeterias.)

Envision means "to foresee; to picture." (I envision an exciting career with many adventures.)

especial/special
> *Especial* means "of great importance; highly distinctive." (The company's free health examination is of especial importance to employees.) *Especially* means "mainly; notably." (The benefits were well received, especially the free medical exmination.)
>
> *Special* means "having some particular quality or some distinctive identity." (This is a special lubricant for typewriter elements.)

essential/necessary
> *Essential* means "basic; indispensable; necessary" and suggests a sense of urgency. (It is essential that we meet our deadline.)
>
> *Necessary* also means "indispensable" but usually sounds less urgent than *essential*. (Your presence is necessary to show our support.)

essentially/substantially
> *Essentially* is used most often to mean "basically." (The new copier is essentially the same as the old one.) The word *essential* implies something indispensable. (Insurance is essential.)
>
> *Substantially* is used in the same way to mean "basically," but the word *substantial* suggests a significant size or quantity. (The company showed a substantial net gain.)

everybody/everyone
> *Everybody* means "every person" and takes a singular verb. (Everybody is there.)
>
> *Everyone* means "everybody" and is the preferred choice of many business writers. Spelled as two words, it refers to each person. (Every one of them is there.)

example/instance/sample
> *Example* means "a particular item that represents a group or type." (The Siamese cat is an example of extreme in-breeding.) It also means "pattern; model." (The technique is an example worth following.)
>
> *Instance* means "a situation tht is used to illustrate something." (In this instance, the strategy failed.)

Sample means "a part; a specimen." (Here is a sample from our new line of merchandise.)

explicit/implicit

Explicit means "clear; fully developed." (The branch manager presented an explicit statement of his objectives.)

Implicit means "understood but not revealed or expressed." (The company's faith in the market was implicit in its actions.) It also means "without doubt or reservation." (He has implicit faith in the new computer system.)

extended/extensive

Extended, a verb, refers to spatial quality and means "spread out; prolonged." (The session will be extended another hour.) It is overused by many business writers to mean "offer" or "send."

Extensive, an adjective, means "having a wide range or extent; broad." (She has extensive knowledge in that scientific field.)

farther/further

Farther refers to physical distance or spatial measurement. (Salespersons travel farther today, thanks to readily available air service.)

Further refers to quantity or degree. This roll of film will go further than I expected.) It also means "to promote." (He hopes to further his career.) Some business writers have stopped using both *farther* and *further* and are using only one of them (usually *further*) for all situations.

fashion/manner/mode

Fashion usually means "a particular style at a particular time." (Her suit is the latest fashion.)

Manner describes "behavior; social conduct." (The director's manners were exemplary.)

Mode means "a particular form of something." (His mode of governing is straightforward and open.)

feasible/possible

Feasible means "capable of being done." (The suggestion sounds feasible to me.)

Possible means "within realistic limits; likely to occur." (An economic upturn next quarter is possible.)

fewer/less

Fewer is used to describe numbers. (Fewer people attended the concert this week.)

Less is used to describe amounts or quantities. (Output was less this month than usual because of the weather.)

first/firstly

First is the preferred form of this adverb and is used to stress points. (First, we have to examine the effect.) Business writers should remember to be consistent in making points: first, second, third (*not* first, secondly, thirdly).

Firstly adds -*ly* unnecessarily.

frequent/recurring

Frequent means "habitual; persistent; occurring at short intervals." (He is a frequent customer.)

Recurring means "occurring again and again; occurring repeatedly." (Her recurring headaches suggest a serious problem.)

gloomy/pessimistic

Gloomy implies "darkness; depression." (She was gloomy following her friend's departure.)

Pessimistic means "an inclination to expect the worse; an inclination to emphasize the negative or adverse aspect." (He was pessimistic about the outcome of the sales campaign.)

good/well

Good, as an adjective, means "praiseworthy; useful; beneficial; free from problems." (She did a good job.)

Well, as an adjective, means "in good health." (She is well.) As an adverb, it means "in a proper manner; with skill." (He handled the job very well.)

grammar/syntax

Grammar means "the study of words and their relationships; the system of inflections and syntax in a language." It is sometimes confused with *usage* which refers more specifically to the rules that apply to written and spoken language.

Syntax refers to the way words are used together to form phrases, clauses, and sentences.

guarantee/guaranty

Guarantee, as a noun, means "an assurance that some condition will be met." (The digital clock had a one-year guarantee.) As a verb, it means "to assure that some debt or obligation will be fulfilled." (The company guaranteed its work.)

Guaranty, as a noun, is used most often in today's business world to mean "the fact of giving security" (contract of guaranty; act of guaranty). As a verb, *guarantee* is preferred over *guaranty.*

handle/manage

Handle means "to control or manage; to deal with" and is preferred over *manage* when physical action is involved. (He handled the controls like an expert.)

Manage also means "to control or handle; to deal with" and is preferred over *handle* when nonphysical action is involved. (She managed the office efficiently.)

happen/occur/transpire

Happen means "to occur by chance." (He happened to be in the neighborhood.)

Occur means "to take place, often unexpectedly" and usually refers to a specific event. (The computer breakdown occurred before closing.)

Transpire means "to pass off; to excrete as a vapor." (The leaves transpired.) Figuratively, it means "to become apparent." (The state of the company became clear as events transpired.)

if/whether

If is used to introduce one condition and often suggests doubt. (I'll meet you at the airport if the weather permits.)

Whether is used to introduce more than one condition. (Her client asked whether she should sue or accept the settlement.)

imagine/suppose

Imagine means "to form a mental image of something." (I like to imagine myself surfing in Hawaii.)

Suppose means "to assume or suspect something." (I suppose you have a contract already drawn up.)

imply/infer
Imply means "to suggest by inference or association." (The report implies that research was inadequate.)

Infer means "to reach a conclusion from facts or circumstances." (The manager inferred from the report that research was inadequate.)

impracticable/impractical/unpractical
Impracticable means "not capable of being used or accomplished." (The plan is impracticable.)

Impractical means "not capable of dealing sensibly or practically with something." (Her approach is impractical.)

Unpractical is an obsolete term for *impracticable*.

incidentally/incidently
Incidentally means "by chance." (Incidentally, I have the latest figures on that.)

Incidently is a misspelling of *incidentally*.

ineffective/ineffectual
Ineffective means "not producing the intended effect; not effective" and often suggests incompetence in some particular area. (He is ineffective as a salesman.)

Ineffectual also means "not producing the intended effect; not effective" and often suggests a general lack of competence. (He is ineffectual.)

ingenious/ingenuous
Ingenious means "resourceful; inventive; clever." (Let me compliment you on your ingenious approach.)

Ingenuous means "innocent; childlike; candid." (The new recruits are ingenuous.)

irony/sarcasm/satire
Irony means "the use of words or statements to express something other than their literal meaning." ("Nice vase," she said pointing to the broken pieces on the floor.)

Sarcasm means "a sharp, critical, derisive, often bitter and cruel form of wit." (I see you made one sale this week—that's twice as many as you made last week, isn't it?)

Satire means "a combination of wit and irony, usually directed toward vice or folly." (The play is a satire about middle-class morality.)

irreversible/irrevocable

Irreversible means "not capable of being changed or reversed" and usually refers to some pattern or course of action. (The trend is irreversible.)

Irrevocable means "not capable of being revoked or repealed" and usually refers to a specific action or statement. (His decision to resign was irrevocable.)

judicial/judicious

Judicial means "of or relating to justice or the judiciary." (He wanted to hear the judicial proceedings.)

Judicious means "having or exercising sound or wise judgment." (She was judicious in the way she used the information.)

know/realize

Know means "to perceive; to understand." (I know a better route.)

Realize means "to accomplish; to grasp fully" and implies a more thorough understanding than *know.* (I realize the implications of our action.)

lack/need/want

Lack, as a noun, means "deficient or absent." (The program suffers from a lack of money.)

Need, as a noun, refers to "a lack of something desirable or useful" and often is used in an emotional context. (The need was for security.)

Want, as a noun, refers to "a lack of something needed or desired." (My wants seem to increase with age.)

As verbs, *lack* suggests a deficiency; *need,* a necessity; and *want,* a desire.

lawful/legal
>*Lawful* means "to be in harmony with some form of law; rightful, ethical." (The directors considered the lawful implications of the amendment.)

>*Legal* means "founded on the law; established by law." (The lottery is legal in New Hampshire.)

libel/slander
>*Libel* means "printed or written defamation causing injury to someone's reputation." (The newspaper account of the scandal was libel.)

>*Slander* means "oral defamation causing injury to someone's reputation." (The remarks he was overheard making about his ex-employer could be considered slander.)

locality/location
>*Locality* means "a specific place" and usually refers to a particular geographic area. (The species is native to that locality.)

>*Location* means "a place of occupancy; a place designated for a special purpose." (The Midwest would be a good location for your sales office.)

luxuriant/luxurious
>*Luxuriant* means "abundant growth." (The plant life is luxuriant here.)

>*Luxurious* means "characterized by self-indulgence or luxury." (The executive suite is luxurious.)

maintain/repair/service
>*Maintain* means "to preserve; to keep in existing condition." (The company doesn't maintain its equipment properly.)

>*Repair* means "to restore; to fix." (They need to repair the mimeograph machine.)

>*Service* also means "to keep in existing condition" and implies inspection as well as repair and maintenance. (The company services all brands of electric typewriters.)

majority/minority/plurality
>*Majority* means "a number greater than one-half of the total."

>*Minority* means "a number less than one-half of the total."

Plurality means "the number of votes in excess of those cast for the closest contender when there are two or more candidates." (Abel received 25,000 votes, Baker received 20,000 votes, and Carson received 4,000 votes; thus Abel had a plurality of 5,000 votes.)

meticulous/scrupulous

Meticulous refers to extreme care in attending to details. (Her work is meticulous.)

Scrupulous refers to high principles and conscientious regard." (He is scrupulous in his dealings with minorities.)

mysterious/mystical/mythical

Mysterious means "something inexplicable; something puzzling" (The chemical's mysterious action produced unpredicted results.)

Mystical means "something having a spiritual or unapparent significance." (The ritual has mystical overtones.)

Mythical means "something imaginary; something involving a myth." (The mythical story about the giant amused the youthful audience.)

official/officious

Official means "relating to an office or position of authority or trust." (Her official duties start tomorrow.)

Officious means "meddlesome." (His actions struck the other employees as officious.)

one's self/oneself

One's self is used less often than *oneself*, except when the emphasis is upon the *self*. (Psychologists say one's self is an amazing entity to be explored endlessly.)

Oneself is the preferred spelling in most general usage. (One has to discipline oneself in any position.)

oral/verbal

Oral means "spoken; by mouth." (They had an oral agreement but nothing in writing.)

Verbal means "consisting of words, written or spoken." (The verbal exercises followed the oral exam; to be more precise, one would say: the written exercises followed the oral exam.)

omission/oversight
   Omission means "something left out; something undone or neglected." (The omission payment was unintentional.)

   Oversight means "an inadvertent omission or error." (Her name was not on the program because of an oversight.)

part/portion/share
   Part means "a subdivision of the whole." (This is one part of the proposal.)

   Portion means "a part or share of something usually intended for a specific purpose." (This portion of the program is reserved for questions and answers.)

   Share means "the part or portion of something belonging to or given by someone." (His share of the estate is being held in trust.)

persons/people
   Persons is often preferred in references to a few individuals or when specific individuals are being discussed. (The president and the treasurer were the only persons there from the board.)

   People is often preferred in references to large groups or indefinite numbers. (The people from Eastern cultures sometimes find it difficult to adjust to Western ways.)

point of view/standpoint/viewpoint
   Point of view, standpoint, and *viewpoint* are used, often overused, interchangeably by business writers today. They refer to an attitude or opinion. (From his point of view, the contract was already null and void.)

practical/practicable
   Practical means "sensible; useful; realistic." (He used a practical approach to the problem.)

   Practicable means "usable; feasible." (It simply is not practicable to complete the project in two weeks.)

prescribed/proscribed
   Prescribed means "laid down as a guide; ordered." (She prescribed complete rest.)

   Proscribed means "condemned; outlawed." (The cult proscribed all Christian literature.)

presumably/supposedly

Presumably means "taken for granted; reasonably assumed to be true." (Presumably he is correct since he ran all of the required tests.)

Supposedly means "believed, sometimes mistakenly, to be true; imagined to be true." (The order to halt production supposedly came from someone in the executive offices.)

principal/principle

Principal, as a noun, means "chief participant or head" (the principal opponent) or "a sum of money." (The mortgage payment including the principal and interest). As an adjective, it means "most important or consequential" (the principal reason).

Principle, a noun, refers to "a rule, doctrine, or assumption" (the principle of universal sovereignty).

proved/proven

Proved is the past tense of *prove*. (They proved their contention.)

Proven is an adjective (the proven method) and a past participle. (The volunteers have proven their loyalty.)

Proved is preferred. (The volunteers have proved their loyalty.)

purposefully/purposely

Purposefully means "with determination; with a purpose." (She purposefully planned her campaign to avoid the holidays.)

Purposely means "intentionally; deliberately." (He purposely avoided the subject.)

qualitative/quantitative

Qualitative refers to quality or essential character. (Their qualitative analysis of the photographs included criteria for clarity and perspective.)

Quantitative refers to quantity or a measurement. (Their quantitative analysis of the containers included measurements of size and volume.)

raise/rear

Raise, as a verb, means "to arouse; to elevate." (Raise the window.) As a noun, it commonly means "an increase in pay." (She got a raise last month.)

Rear, as a verb, means "to raise upright" (the animal reared) or "to bring up a child" (reared four children). Informally: one also *raises* children.

reaction/reply/response
Reaction means "a response to stimuli." (The injection caused a violent reaction.) It should not be used to mean "attitude, viewpoint, feeling, or response."

Reply means "a response in words." (She sent her reply by messenger.)

Response is "a reply; an answer." (The client's response was positive.)

redundant/superfluous
Redundant means "more than necessary; repetitive" and usually refers to wordiness in oral and written communication. (That paragraph is redundant.)

Superfluous means "exceeding what is needed" but the emphasis is upon something useless or unnecessary rather than repetitive. (Many of his proposals are superfluous.)

reported/reputed
Reported means "made known." (They reported the error immediately.)

Reputed means "considered; believed; supposed." (The company is reputed to be a leader in the industry.)

shall/will
Shall, traditionally, is used in the first person to express future time. (I shall be happy to go.) Some authorities believe *shall* sounds stuffy and snobbish and prefer to use *will*.

Will, traditionally, is used in the second or third person to express future time. (He will be happy to go.) Contemporary usage shows an increasing preference for *will* in all instances (I will, you will, he/she will, they will.)

stationary/stationery
Stationary, an adjective, means "fixed, immobile." (The mountain peak is stationary.)

Stationery, a noun, means "writing paper and related office supplies." (It's time to order new stationery.)

strain/stess

Strain, as a verb, means "to misuse; to filter; to stretch beyond belief; to overexert." (He strained his muscles.) As a noun, it means "excessive exertion or tension." (No strain on his heart was evident.)

Stress, as a verb, means "to accent; to emphasize." (He stressed the danger involved.) As a noun, it means "pressure; tension." (She suffered great stress during the competition.)

subconscious/unconscious

Subconscious means "mental activities of which one is not conscious or aware." (They wondered what subconscious motive he had for provoking his employer.)

Unconscious means "loss of consciousness or awareness." (She was unconscious for an hour after the accident.)

systematize/systemize

Systematize is the more familiar expression meaning "to arrange systematically; to put in order." (The committee needs to systematize its work.)

Systemize, although used less often, means the same as *systematize.*

that/which

That refers to persons, animals, or things and should be used in restrictive clauses where the clause introduced by *that* is essential to explain the preceding information. (The group that won last year came in first again.) The clause "that won last year" provides essential information about the group. It should *not* be set off with commas.

Which refers to animals and things and should be used in nonrestrictive clauses where the clause introduced by *which* is not essential for the reader to understand the meaning of the other information in the sentence. (The robin, which flies south in the winter, has a colorful orange breast.) The clause "which flies south in the winter" is not essential for the reader to understand that the robin has an orange breast. It *should* be set off with commas.

trace/vestige
> *Trace* means "evidence of something that has passed." (She could find no trace of the file.)
>
> *Vestige* means "a visible sign; an actual mark of something that has passed." (The ruins are the last vestige of the ancient city.)

toward/towards
> *Toward* is a shorter, and thus preferred, version of the word meaning "in the direction of; approaching" (moving toward the finish line).
>
> *Towards* is a variation of *toward*.

varied/various
> *Varied* means "diverse; with numerous forms." (The logos on business letterheads are varied.)
>
> *Various* means "dissimilar; separate; different." (The memo was sent to various divisions in the company.)

viable/workable
> *Viable* means "capable of existence." (The new company is a viable entity.)
>
> *Workable* means "practicable; feasible; capable of working or succeeding." (The plan seems workable to me.)

want/wish
> *Want* suggests a need or longing. (I want that promotion.)
>
> *Wish* is used more often to suggest hope as well as desire. (I wish I had more money.)

who/whom
> *Who* is in the subjective case. (The man who is in charge will be here shortly.) *Who* is the subject of *is*.
>
> *Whom* is in the objective case. (The man whom he left in charge will be here shortly.) *Whom* is the object of *left*.

3 SPELLING, PUNCTUATION, AND CAPITALIZATION

When you think about spelling, punctuation, and capitalization, you probably think about rules and more rules. Most likely, though, you don't think about these things at all. After all, you learned how to spell, punctuate, and capitalize in grade school. How many business people have time for such trivial matters now? Besides, what more is there to know? A lot! Incorrect, inconsistent, and careless habits in these three areas can mar the appearance and readability of your written messages and detract from your reputation as an accomplished professional. Precisely because so many business people never think about spelling, punctuation, and capitalization, they make glaring mistakes and produce written communication that looks very unprofessional.

Dividing Words Properly

Correct word division must be low on the list of priorities for most business writers, because business messages are replete with errors in hyphenation and end-of-line breaks. Apparently the problem filters down from the management to the clerical level (or is it the other way around?). Readers of messages that come out of a business office get the feeling that either no one knows how to divide a word or no one cares. Although both general dictionaries and spelling dictionaries show where a word may be divided, few people take time to consult a dictionary about word division. Even fewer people know the basic rules for dividing words and the preferred practices when a choice exists.

Have you ever received a letter or report that was overloaded with hyphens? Too many hyphens will spoil the appearance of your written

73

communication, and numerous end-of-line breaks will slow the recipient's reading speed and comprehension. Before deciding *where* to break a word, it pays to ask whether the division is even necessary. If it is, the next question is where to make the break.

Anyone who prepares written communication should observe a few general guidelines that will help readers digest a message with minimal interruption and distraction: do not divide a word unless it is absolutely necessary; do not divide the last word in a paragraph or the last word on a page (except in legal documents); do not divide words at the end of two or more successive lines; do not divide words at points where the divisions may confuse readers. But if you must break a word, follow the standard rules and preferred practices for correct word division described below.

Syllabication is the key to correct word division. Words should be divided only between syllables, although not all syllable breaks are acceptable places to divide a word. This is often where the trouble begins. General dictionaries and spelling dictionaries mark the syllables in each word, and many business people send written messages with words divided at *any* syllable break shown in a dictionary. Skilled writers recognize that certain points are preferred for breaking a word.

Pronunciation is often your best clue to syllabication. In the following words pronunciation makes the difference:

proj-ect (a plan)

pro-ject (to throw forward)

pre-sent (to introduce to another)

pres-ent (now existing)

Pronunciation can help in other doubtful cases too:

knowl-edge (*not* know-ledge)

hypoc-risy (*not* hypo-crisy)

Some words appear to have more than one syllable, but pronunciation makes it easy to see why they are treated as one-syllable words and thus must not be divided:

through (*not* th-rough)

shipped (*not* ship-ped)

Some authorities say that no word of less than six letters should be divided:

carat (*not* car-at)

silo (*not* si-lo)

Some words clearly have more than one syllable and six or more letters, but they nevertheless should not be divided. The following words begin or end with a one-letter syllable. Particular writers never divide a word before or after a single letter:

aboard (*not* a-board)

hys-te-ria (*not* hysteri-a)

Careful writers do not divide a word unless three or more characters including the hyphen are on the top line:

re-tract (re-)

de-note (de-)

Three or more characters including punctuation must also be carried to the bottom line:

hook-up, (up,) *but not* hook-up (up)

later-al: (al:) *but not* later-al (al)

Treat prefixes and suffixes as single syllables and do not divide them. Instead, divide a word *after* the prefix and *before* the suffix:

inter-office (*not* in-teroffice)

anti-nuclear (*not* an-tinuclear)

pos-sible (*not* possi-ble)

cap-able (*not* capa-ble)

When a consonant is doubled before adding an -*ing* ending, break the word between the two consonants:

occur-ring (*not* occurr-ing)

travel-ling (*not* travell-ing)

Do not confuse these examples with words that end in a double consonant. The word *travel* does not end in a double consonant, but a word like *dwell* or *spell* does. Break such words after the double consonant:

  spell-ing (*not* spel-ling)

  dwell-ing (*not* dwel-ling)

  Few business writers pay any attention to single syllables within a word; they divide before or after the single syllable without exception. Editors often point to this as the most common disregard of preferred practices in word division. Particular writers always divide a word *after* a single syllable:

  criti-cize (*not* crit-icize)

  manu-facture (*not* man-ufacture)

  Some words are already hyphenated. Such compound words should be divided only at the hyphen:

  vice-president (*not* vice-presi-dent)

  all-attentive (*not* all-atten-tive)

  Proper names should not be divided if possible. First and last names of persons should be separated only between the two names:

  Jeanne / Hudson (*not* Jeanne Hud-son)

  R. V. / Mason (*not* R. / V. Mason)

  Figures are best left alone but may be divided at the comma if necessary:

  1,702,-600,000 (*not* 1,70-2,600,000)

  Contractions such as *don't* and abbreviations such as *UNESCO* should not be divided. Abbreviations used with figures should not be separated from the figures:

  9:30 P.M. (*not* 9:30 / P.M.)

Other obvious word groups should not be separated either:

  page 4 (*not* page / 4)

  160 miles (*not* 160 / miles)

But if it is essential to separate some word groups, observe the following rules. Dates may be separated between day and year:

August 5, / 1982 (*not* August / 5, 1982)

Numbered or lettered lists may be separated before the number or letter:

the following: / (1) today (*not* the following: (1) / today)

Addresses may be separated between words in the address but not between numbers and words:

1600 Pennsylvania / Avenue (*not* 1600 / Pennsylvania Avenue)

When a dash falls where a sentence must be divided, keep the dash on the top line:

beginning this week—   (*not* beginning this week
if time permits   —if time permits)

Word division is not the only purpose for which hyphens are used. The following section describes the other important uses of the hyphen.

Punctuating for Clarity

Without punctuation, some words would run together in an incoherent tangle. Punctuation is meant to help your readers follow and understand your messages quickly and easily. But too much punctuation or misused and misplaced punctuation are just as bad as not enough punctuation. A business writer must be able to judge what is enough to make a message clear and readable without being so much that the reader's flow of thought is interrupted every few words.

The trend is toward minimal punctuation, for example: less use of the comma after brief introductory phrases and words such as "In 1981" or "In the United States" and less use of the comma to separate two short, closely related clauses connected by a conjunction. But many business writers still *over*punctuate their messages. Often they overpunctuate because they use long, cumbersome, rambling sentences composed of numerous isolated phrases and interjections:

The directors' meeting convened in the afternoon, with twelve directors present, at the Holiday Inn, following the Executive Committee meeting in the morning, at which time the three officers worked on the agenda, after the president presented his proposal for Wednesday's conference, and upon the committee's recommendation, the directors moved immediately into a discussion of the conference program.

How much proper punctuation helps such a disaster is debatable. A rambling, awkward sentence is still a rambling, awkward sentence. Effective business messages combine all aspects of writing, and proper punctuation is one of many aids to clarity, not a solution for other weaknesses.

The principal marks of punctuation are the apostrophe, bracket, colon, comma, dash, ellipsis, exclamation point, hyphen, parenthesis, period, question mark, quotation mark, and semicolon. Each mark is described below with examples of common uses in business writing.

Apostrophe

Use the apostrophe to show possession, omission, and some plurals. To show plurals, use the apostrophe and s:

p's and q's

2's and 3's

c.o.d.'s

But omit the apostrophe if the s alone can be used without confusion:

1980s

80s

YMCAs

To show possession, add an apostrophe and an s to a singular word, but omit the s if the word already ends in ss. Add an apostrophe alone to a plural word that already ends in s:

candidate's slogan

boss' orders

someone's coat

executives' lounge

two weeks' work

With names, add an apostrophe and an s to a singular word and an apostrophe alone to a plural word:

Joe Adams's car

the Adamses' house

Use the apostrophe to distinguish between joint and separate possession:

Bill and Don's proposal (joint)

Bill's and Don's proposals (separate)

To show omission, use the apostrophe alone:

we'll (we will)

it's (it is)

'80s (1980s)

Brackets

Use brackets to enclose comments and corrections that are not part of quoted material and to enclose parenthetical comments within parentheses:

According to the director, "The XL-722 [replacing the XL-721] will be ready for marketing this fall."

The auditorium had standing room only (reminiscent of the candidates' last [1976] controversial confrontation).

Colon

Use the colon after salutations in business letters; to separate dates and pages and cities and publishers in citations; to show ratios and time; and to indicate something such as a list, tabulation, quotation, or example. But do not use a colon after verbs such as *are* unless a formal list follows:

Dear Mr. Wright:

Business Journal 2 (1981): 17

Windfall Profits Tax (New York: Business Publications, Inc., 1981)

4:2:1

8:25 A.M.

The following are examples of modern typefaces: Press Roman, Spartan, and Helvetica.

Some writers also use the colon to indicate a pause between two closely related sentences not linked by a conjunction:

This is the situation: we have to trim $20,000 from the budget.

The company had one objective: it wanted to outdistance all major competitors.

Comma

Use the comma to separate three or more words or phrases in a series and the clauses of a compound sentence. Use a comma to show the omission of words. Set off *nonrestrictive clauses* (those clauses that add something that is not essential to the sentence) with commas. Set off introductory and transitional words and phrases, words in apposition, parenthetical expressions, or quoted material with commas:

He called clients in New York, Los Angeles, and Detroit. (series comma)

Ten employees volunteered to work on Thanksgiving last year; four, this year. (omission of words)

The shop, which is closed on Mondays, is located near the bus terminal. (nonrestrictive clause)

After you finish the survey, please send the forms to the data-processing center. (introductory phrase)

It is, however, too late to call now. (transitional word)

The school's president, Andrew Smith, will speak at the dinner meeting. (appositive)

The sound, of course, is amplified in this room. (parenthetical expression)

"We will likely see a decline in sales this quarter," he said, "but the decline should be followed by an increase next quarter." (quoted material)

In 1980, 4,300 persons were registered to vote in Ward 2. (numbers)

The day after, he arrived by train. (to prevent misreading)

Although commas are essential for clarity in numerous situations, writers often use them unnecessarily. Too many commas, or commas where they are not needed, slow the reader's pace and give the writing a jerky, staccato effect. The following sentences should not use the commas shown in parentheses:

Yesterday (,) it was 80 degrees (,) and today it is 40 degrees.

The customer said (,) that she wanted a refund.

His brother (,) Allen (,) arrived last week. (He may have more than one brother; since *Allen* is therefore necessary to indicate *which* brother, it is essential to the sentence and should not be set off by commas.)

In 1978 (,) the company issued its first newsletter.

Afterwards (,) we stopped (,) at the Katz Lounge (,) for a drink.

Dash

Use the dash to show a sudden interruption or to set off explanatory clauses emphatically. But do not combine the dash with other punctuation marks. A comma followed by a dash, for instance, is out of style. The main problem business writers have with the dash is deciding whether to set off or introduce a clause with commas or the dash. Some writers incorrectly use a dash for every pause in thought and before and after every nonrestrictive clause. Unless special emphasis is needed, commas would be much more appropriate in most cases. The following examples show some legitimate uses for the dash:

Paris, Brussels, Amsterdam, Cologne—these are the principal cities he will visit in Europe.

The new merchandise—if you can call it new—has the same basic design as before.

Phil Baxter—he transferred from the southern office—is going to head the new department.

Work—is that all you ever think about?

Ellipses

Use ellipses to show the omission of words. Three dots are used to show words omitted in the middle of a sentence. Four dots are used to show words, sentences, and paragraphs omitted at the end of a sentence. Follow these examples for spacing around ellipses:

The advertisement stated: "If you are not fully satisfied . . . your money will be refunded in full."

Construction began . . . in April, according to a company spokesperson, but had come to a halt by June. . . . By July eighty employees were out of work. . . .

Exclamation Point

Use the exclamation point to show strong feeling, surprise, or irony. But do not use this mark if the words alone or other punctuation would convey your feelings just as well. Irony, for example, is usually obvious without special punctuation. Unnecessary use and overuse of the exclamation point causes it to lose its effectiveness. Here are some examples of legitimate use:

Sale! 30 Percent Off All Items!

Oh, no! How could this have happened?

Hurry up! The storm is getting worse!

Hyphen

Use the hyphen to divide words at the end of a line (see the section "Dividing Words Properly") and to separate compound words. Use hyphens in spelled out fractional numbers and telephone numbers and to separate certain street numbers. Do not hyphenate adverbs ending in -ly (highly) plus an adjective (skilled) or participle. Do not hyphenate compound adjective forms that follow a noun, except all- compounds, self- compounds, and half- compounds. Some adjective forms are never hyphenated, before or after a noun, particularly well-known compounds such as civil service and compounds with percentages such as 5 percent. For instance:

a well-built house

the house is well built

highly skilled technician

five-foot ladder

55 percent reduction

social security increase

an all-powerful directive

the directive is all-powerful

a self-educated man

the man is self-educated

two-thirds

twenty-three-year-old woman

the woman is twenty-three years old

A noun-plus-noun combination is always hyphenated:

manager-director

city-state

Vice-compounds are usually hyphenated:

vice-president

Quasi noun compounds are not hyphenated, but *quasi-* adjective compounds are hyphenated before and after a noun:

the quasi corporation

the quasi-public corporation

the corporation is quasi-public

Many business offices use the suspended hyphen for measurements. Notice the spacing around the hyphens in these examples:

8½- by 11-inch paper

3- by 5-inch cards

Hyphenate words formed with prefixes preceding a proper name. Most other words formed with prefixes are spelled closed:

anti-American

antiwar

pro-European

prolabor

pre-Columbian

preeminent

The *-like* suffix words are hyphenated when the compound is formed from a proper name or from another word already ending in *ll*:

Soviet-like defense

skull-like pendant

catlike movements

When you must consult a dictionary about the use of hyphens, pick a recent edition that shows current trends such as writing most words with prefixes closed. Or consult the latest edition of a stylebook such as *A Manual of Style* (University of Chicago Press).

Parentheses

Use parentheses to enclose incidental comments and figures or letters in lists run into the text:

The study discusses government regulation of pesticides (page 41).

The budget passed (with minimal revision) by a vote of four to one.

His birthday is May 12 (?) and her birthday is June 4.

(1) using brackets, (2) using parentheses, (3) using dashes

Period

Use the period to end a sentence, after numbers and letters in a vertical list, after some abbreviations, and as decimals in numbers (also see the section "Ellipses," page 82):

The report is finished.

a. Electricity

b. Water

Mich.

$22.98

Question Marks

Use the question mark to end a direct question and to show doubt:

Are you coming?

Will you be free Wednesday? Friday?

The terminal input leads are coded green (?) and the output leads are coded red.

Quotation Marks

Use quotation marks to enclose precise quotations of written or spoken material, but do not enclose *yes* or *no* except in direct discourse. Use single quotation marks for a quotation within a quotation. Enclose titles of articles, unpublished works, essays, TV shows, short poems, and short musical works in quotation marks. (But underscore titles of movies, books, periodicals, plays, long poems, works of art, and long musical works. In typeset material, underscored words are set in italics.) Do not use quotation marks when the name of a speaker or writer introduces the quoted words. Do not enclose slang in quotation marks and do not enclose words following the expression *so-called* in quotation marks. Do not enclose indented material typed as an extract in quotation marks:

"The projector is working fine," he said. "It's the filmstrip that is damaged."

"According to this brochure," she said, reading aloud, " 'the controls are self-regulating.' "

When I asked him if he would like to come, he said yes.

Read the chapter "Office Efficiency" before the next class.

Jason "Wild Bill" Chandler

Ms. Jones: Yes, I am employed there.

the so-called kissing bandit

He was uptight the first day in his new position.

Semicolon

Use the semicolon (rather than a comma) to separate clauses that do not have a connecting conjunction. Use the semicolon to separate items in a series that already have commas:

We need to streamline our filing systems; in fact, we need to streamline all of our office procedures.

Copies of the telegram were sent to representatives in Portland, Maine; Des Moines, Iowa; Dallas, Texas; and Sacramento, California.

The project leaders are Jack Lewis, who is starting his fifth year with us; Jeanne Martin, who joined the company this fall; and Dennis Hart, who just transferred from our New Orleans office.

Punctuation in business messages varies with the writer. One person might prefer to use dashes to set off a parenthetical expression; another person might prefer to enclose the remark in parentheses. Aside from such matters of personal taste, successful business writers observe the rules described above. They do not overuse any mark of punctuation; they use only what is essential to state their message clearly and accurately. They punctuate for clarity.

Capitalizing Do's and Don'ts

Just as the trend is toward minimal use of punctuation, the trend also is toward minimal use of capitalization. A lot of words that once were capitalized are now *lowercased* (written with an initial small letter instead of an initial capital letter). Previously one always capitalized references to the president of the United States (the President). Now titles such as *president*, *attorney general*, and *chief justice* are no longer capitalized unless they precede a proper name (President Reagan).

Capitalization affects the appearance of your writing, and in the business world, appearances matter. No one wants to send out messages that look out of date. You may disagree with contemporary usage or prefer traditional usage. But anyone who fails to keep up with changing styles in spelling, punctuation, and capitalization runs the risk of appearing uninformed and behind the times, an image that most business people want to avoid. The following rules are important when appearances count. Even when you opt for a different style, one thing is always essential: consistency. Whether you want to write *president* with a capital or lowercase *p*, follow whatever style you choose consistently.

The following guidelines for capitalization show examples of terms in thirteen principal areas of usage: education; geography; government and politics; history; holidays, festivals, and seasons; the judiciary; listings and outlines; the military; numbers; proper nouns; religion; titles of persons; and titles of works.

Education

Capitalize the official names of departments, schools, and colleges:

New York University

the university

Franklin Pierce High School

the high school

Department of Political Science

the political science department

Capitalize the names of classes and the official titles of courses:

Freshman Class

a freshman

Economics 101

an economics course

Capitalize degrees and honors that are part of a name or title:

Bernard O. Winslow Fellowship

the fellowship

Jonathan Davis, Ph.D.

Martha Bigelow Howe, Master of Arts

the bachelor of arts degree

Geography

Capitalize the divisions or major parts of the world, the divisions or major regions of continents and countries, and official topographical names:

Middle East

Pacific Coast region

North Atlantic states

Western world

the West (region, U.S.)

western (direction, locality)

the Orient

oriental culture

North Africa

northern Africa

Nile Delta

the delta

Black Forest

Pacific Ocean

Mississippi River

Mississippi and Arkansas rivers

Capitalize popular names of regions and localities:

East Side (New York)

the Loop (Chicago)

Bay Area (San Francisco)

Deep South (U.S.)

the Village (New York)

New World

Foggy Bottom (Washington, D.C.)

Government and Politics

Capitalize the official titles of acts, bills, laws, amendments, and constitutions:

Wagner Act

the act

Rogers Bill

the bill

First Amendment (U.S. Constitution)

the amendment (state or U.S.)

Georgia State Constitution

the constitution (state)

United States Constitution

the Constitution (U.S.)

Capitalize the names of political parties and the offical titles of administrative, legislative, and deliberative bodies:

Communist party

Communists

communism

the party

the Left

left wing

left-wingers

the Security Council (UN)

the council

Birmingham Board of Education

the board of education

General Assembly of Illinois

Massachusetts legislature

Parliament (British)

parliamentary

Congress (U.S.)

congressional

Senate Finance Committee

the committee

House of Representatives

the House

Capitalize political divisions or units when they follow a name or when they are an accepted part of it:

Madison County

the county of Madison

Iowa State

the state of Iowa

New York City

the city of New York

Fourth Ward

the ward

the Union (U.S.)

federal government

History

Capitalize the official names of important events, documents, early cultural periods, major geological periods, and movements derived from proper names:

World War I

Declaration of Independence

Pliocene epoch

Iron Age

space age

colonial period (U.S.)

twentieth century

Platonism

surrealism

Holidays, Festivals, and Seasons

Capitalize the names of religious seasons, religious and secular holidays, and calendar months and days of the week:

Twelfth Day

Passover

New Year's Day

election day

September

Tuesday

autumn

winter solstice

The Judiciary

Capitalize the official titles of courts and job titles when they precede a proper name, and capitalize all important words in legal cases:

United States Supreme Court

the Court (U.S. Supreme)

Houston Court of Civil Appeals

the court of civil appeals

Ohio Court of Common Pleas

the family court

American Bar Association

the bar

P. Jefferson Jones v. *Department of Public Works*

the *Jones* Case

Justice Burns

Mr. Justice Burns

the justice

Listings and Outlines

Capitalize the first word in each item of a list or outline:

I. Quotation marks

    A. Punctuating quotations

        1. Long quotations

        2. Short quotations

The Military

Capitalize military titles preceding a proper name and the full names of military groups, wars, craft and vessels, and awards:

Donald O. Smith, commander

Commander Donald O. Smith

the commander

L. T. Maxwell, Admiral of the Fleet (Admiral of the Fleet and General of the Army are always capitalized to avoid ambiguity)

Allied forces

National Guard

the guard

United States Coast Guard

the Coast Guard

Royal Air Force

British air force

United States Army

the army

Pacific Fleet

the fleet

Viet Nam War

the war

S.S. *United States*

ICBM

Purple Heart

Numbers

Capitalize sums of money in checks and formal documents, names or classifications with numbers, and formal names containing numbers:

One Hundred Dollars ($100)

Twelfth Precinct

Ward 12

Local No. 23

U.S. Route 81

Seventh Avenue

Third Reich

Eighty-ninth Congress

six o'clock

five people

nineteenth century

12 pounds

Proper Nouns

Capitalize the names of particular persons, places, and things, including peoples, races, tribes; epithets; fictitious names; trade names;

and words that are personified (also see the rules for proper names in the above sections):

Ambassador Otis Steiner

North America

the Capitol (U.S.)

Champs Elysées

Edison Packing Company

the company

Great Depression

the depression

Milky Way

aurora borealis

Hodgkins disease

pneumonia

Pacific standard time

eastern standard time

Orientals

Indo-Europeans

blacks

aborigines

Romans

roman numerals

Prince of Wales

the First Lady

Uncle Sam

Coca-Cola

soft drink

Angel of Death

Don Quixote

quixotic

Religion

Capitalize names for the Bible; books and divisions of the Bible; other sacred religious works; references to the Deity in formal or religious writing; special events, rites, and services; and official names of specific churches:

Bible

the Good Book

biblical

King James Version (Bible)

Psalms

the Scriptures

the Gospels

the gospel truth

New Testament

Talmud

talmudic

Heavenly Father

Greek gods

Holy Communion

Resurrection

the Mass (the eucharistic sacrament)

high mass (an individual celebration)

baptism

bar mitzvah

Protestant church

Third Presbyterian Church of Lewisville

Titles of Persons

Capitalize titles when they precede a person's name:

Vice-President Bush

George Bush, vice-president of the United States

the vice-president

Major Nollin

the major

Rabbi Feldman

the rabbi

Senator Jack Orestes

the senator

Queen Elizabeth

Her Majesty

the queen

the Queen Mother

Daniel Curtis Watson, second earl of Devonshire

the earl of Devonshire

Professor Joseph Viotelli

the sociologist Joseph Viotelli

Dr. Bette McCade

the physician Bette McCade

Titles of Works

Capitalize all important words, including verbs, in titles of written works, musical compositions, paintings and sculptures, television and radio programs, and motion pictures:

Word Origins: The Romance of Language (book)

Journal of Business Economics (periodical)

"McCall Theory of Inventory Mobility" (dissertation)

"Charlie's Angels" (TV show)

the *Emperor* Concerto, Piano Concerto no. 5 (musical composition)

The Thinker (sculpture)

The Divine Comedy (poem)

Because of the trend away from excessive capitalization, business writers often wonder whether to capitalize or not to capitalize in specific instances. Some confusion and doubt is inevitable whenever an obvious change in style like this is taking place nationwide. This section has covered the common areas of concern to business writers; for special problems, consult a current dictionary or the latest edition of a stylebook such as A *Manual of Style* (University of Chicago Press). If you need a general guideline, remember that you are safer leaning toward *under*capitalization rather than *over*capitalization. No matter which way you go, you must *be consistent* to avoid the appearance of carelessness and lack of pride in your work.

Using Abbreviations in Business Writing

The pressure of time prompts many business people to look for shortcuts in preparing written messages. Abbreviations are the business writer's shorthand for note taking and writing rough drafts. But should abbreviations also be used in the final copy of letters, reports, and other communications? Most authorities say no (with a few exceptions), not in business letters or any other nontechnical business communication.

Abbreviations are often necessary and appropriate in the many specialized areas of science and technology. But generally, abbreviations are discouraged in nontechnical business writing, except for use in footnotes and bibliographies and in tables, charts, and other illustrations. Thus you would never send out a letter with the abbreviation *admin.* for *administration* or *Jan.* for *January* or *in.* for *inch.* However, a few abbreviated words are seldom spelled out: personal and professional titles such as *Mr., Ms., Mrs., Dr.*; scholarly degrees such as *Ph.D., Sc.D.*; and time-date abbreviations such as A.M., P.M. and A.D., B.C.

So much disagreement exists concerning the use of capital letters and periods in abbreviations that it is difficult for a business person to decide who is right. For "collect on delivery," should you write *c.o.d.* or *C.O.D.* or *COD?* For "millimeter," should you write *mm* or *mm.?* Often the answer depends upon which dictionary or which other authority you are following. Use the authority you prefer but *be logical* and *consistent* in using abbreviations. If you use the small letters *a.c.* for "alternating current," you should not use the capital letters *D.C.* for "direct current"; If you write *mm.* for "millimeter" with a period, you should not write *cm* for "centimeter" without a period.

Deciding *what* to abbreviate may be more difficult than deciding *how* to abbreviate it. The following are examples of words that should never be abbreviated in the main body of your business messages (some of these abbreviations are used in supporting material such as footnotes and tables):

abr. (abridged)

art. (article)

col. (column)

cont. (continued)

dept. (department)

dir. (director)

div. (division)

engr. (engineer)

esp. (especially)

ex. (example)

hdqrs. (headquarters)

incl. (inclusive)

med. (median)

mgmt. (management)

mgr. (manager)

misc. (miscellaneous)

nat. (national)

org. (organization)

par. (paragraph)

pub. (publication)

sec. (secretary)

treas. (treasurer)

univ. (university)

yr. (year)

Government agencies and other organizations are often abbreviated in both technical and nontechnical material. In general business writing, spell out the name of the organization the first time you mention it, for example: *National Labor Relations Board (NLRB)*. A few organizations are so well known by their abbreviated names that you need not spell them in full the first time, for example: *YMCA* and *AFL-CIO*. Here are some examples of abbreviations of organizations used in nontechnical as well as technical business writing:

AEC (Atomic Energy Commission)

AFL-CIO (American Federation of Labor and Congress of Industrial Organizations)

AT&T (American Telephone & Telegraph)

CAB (Civil Aeronautics Board)

CARE (Cooperative for American Remittances to Europe)

CIA (Central Intelligence Agency)

DAR (Daughters of the American Revolution)

FBI (Federal Bureau of Investigation)

FCC (Federal Communications Commission)

FDIC (Federal Deposit Insurance Corporation)

FHA (Federal Housing Authority)

IBM (International Business Machines)

NAACP (National Association for the Advancement of Colored People)

NATO (North Atlantic Treaty Organization)

NLRB (National Labor Relations Board)

NOW (National Organization for Women)

PTA (Parent-Teacher Association)

RCA (Radio Corporation of America)

ROTC (Reserve Officers' Training Corps)

SEATO (Southeast Asia Treaty Organization)

SEC (Securities and Exchange Commission)

UN (United Nations)

UNICEF (United Nations Children's Fund)

USIA (United States Information Agency)

YMCA/YWCA (Young Men's/Women's Christian Association)

Spell out states in general business writing. In the inside addresses of your business letters, you should use the appropriate two-letter state postal abbreviations. In footnotes or tables, you should abbreviate the states in their traditional form:

Ala. AL	Mont. MT
Alaska AK	Nebr. NE
Ariz. AZ	Nev. NV
Ark. AR	N.H. NH
Calif. CA	N.J. NJ
Colo. CO	N.Mex. NM
Conn. CT	N.Y. NY
Del. DE	N.C. NC
D.C. DC	N.Dak. ND
Fla. FL	Ohio OH
Ga. GA	Okla. OK
Hawaii HI	Oreg. OR
Idaho ID	Pa. PA
Ill. IL	R.I. RI
Ind. IN	S.C. SC
Iowa IA	S.Dak. SD
Kans. KS	Tenn. TN
Ky. KY	Tex. TX
La. LA	Utah UT
Maine ME	Vt. VT
Md. MD	Va. VA
Mass. MA	Wash. WA
Mich. MI	W.Va. WV
Minn. MN	Wis. WI
Miss. MS	Wyo. WY
Mo. MO	

Contemporary English-language usage includes a growing list of acronyms such as *SALT* (Strategic Arms Limitation Talks) and popular expressions such as UFO (unidentified flying objects). You may use acronyms such as *SALT* in most business writing, but treat many of the popular expressions such as *UFO* with caution. Some authorities insist that most of these popular expressions usually should be spelled out in general business text and always in formal writing. The following are examples of popular abbreviations:

ASAP (as soon as possible)

AV (audiovisual)

ESP (extrasensory perception)

GNP (gross national product)

MP (military police)

IQ (intelligence quotient)

M.O. (money order)

P.O. (post office)

PR (public relations)

R&D (research and development)

RR (railroad)

SOP (standard operating procedure)

TB (tuberculosis)

TLC (tender loving care)

TV (television)

VIP (very important person)

In the few cases where prominent persons are referred to by initials, do not use periods: *JFK* and *FDR*. When titles such as *Reverend* and *Honorable* are preceded by the word *the*, spell out the title: *the Reverend James Becker*. Otherwise, abbreviate the title: *Rev. James Becker*. Spell out titles preceding a surname alone: *Captain Rogers*. Otherwise, you may usually abbreviate the title: *Capt. Henry Rogers*. Never use the abbreviation *Esq.* with another title (*not* Mr. Michel Skinner, Esq.). You may usually abbreviate scholarly degrees and similar titles that follow a name: *Samuel Feldman, LL.D.* You may abbreviate words such as *company* in footnotes and bibliographies: *New*

York Publications Co. Spell out prefixes of geographic names in text material: *Saint Louis.* Except for *USSR,* spell out the names of countries in text material: *United States.* In informal communication, you may abbreviate *United States* when it is used as an adjective: *U.S. institutions.*

The following are examples of abbreviations used in specialized writing:

a (ampere)

A/C (account current)

a.k.a. (also known as)

bbl (barrels)

B/E (bill of exchange)

bl (bales)

B/L (bill of lading)

B/R (bills receivable)

B/S (bill of sale)

C (Celsius)

cg (centigram)

CIF (cost, insurance, and freight)

cm (centimeter)

c/o (care of)

COD (cash, or collect, on delivery)

cwt. (hundredweight)

EOM (end of month)

ETA (estimated time of arrival)

F (Fahrenheit)

FAS (free alongside ship)

FOB (free on board)

g (gram)

gr. (gross)

kg (kilogram)

km (kilometer)

l (liter)

LCL (less-than-carload lot)

m (meter)

M (1,000)

ml (milliliter)

mm (millimeter)

n/30 (net in 30 days)

NA (not applicable or not available)

nt. wt. (net weight)

OS (out of stock)

PO (purchase order)

POE (port of entry)

rpm (revolutions per minute)

/S/ (signed)

SO (shipping order)

Most business people have to check at least some of the abbreviations they use for spelling, capitalization, and punctuation. For general business writing, any modern dictionary will do. The specialized dictionaries (for example for medicine or engineering) are often more useful to special-interest business writers. An excellent source for any business writer is *The Complete Dictionary of Abbreviations*, by Robert J. Schwartz (Thomas Y. Crowell Co.).

Learning to Spell Correctly

Everyone has been reading about the shocking rise in functional illiteracy in the United States, about the increasing number of students leaving our schools unable to read or write well enough to use these skills in later employment. But the problem is not restricted to the young. Spelling errors are common in business communications too, whether they result from carelessness or ignorance. No matter what the cause is, misspelled words cloud a business person's professional reputation and the image of the organization he or she represents.

Learning to spell correctly is essential for anyone who writes any form of business communication.

Several spelling aids are available to business writers. You can always look up a troublesome word in the dictionary, and you should take time to proofread everything you write. You can also learn a few simple rules described below to help you avoid some of the common errors in spelling.

Plurals

Most singular nouns can be made plural by adding -s:

    book/books

    car/cars

When a word ends in *y* preceded by a consonant, change the *y* to *i* and add -es: When the *y* is preceded by a vowel, add -s:

    century/centuries

    attorney/attorneys

When a word ends in *ch*, *sh*, *ss*, or *x*, add -es:

    church/churches

    dish/dishes

    class/classes

    box/boxes

When a word ends in *f*, *ff*, or *fe*, add -s or change the *f* to *v* and add -es (no clear-cut rule exists to tell you when to change the *f* to *v*):

    roof/roofs

    cliff/cliffs

    safe/safes

    loaf/loaves

    wife/wives

    shelf/shelves

When a word ends in *o* preceded by a vowel, add -s. When the word ends in *o* preceded by a consonant, add *-es* in most cases, add *-s* in a few cases, and add either *-s* or *-es* in a few cases:

folio/folios

hero/heroes

memo/memos

zero/zeros/zeroes/

To make a compound noun plural, add *-s* to the most important word. In a few cases, both words take *-s*. When a word ends in *-ful*, add *-s* to the end of the compound:

editor in chief/editors in chief

president-elect/presidents-elect

right-of-way/rights-of-way

trade union/trade unions

bill of lading/bills of lading

notary public/notaries public

woman volunteer/women volunteers

coat of arms/coats of arms

Certain words become plural by a change in spelling rather than by adding *-s*. Other words have the same form for both singular and plural:

child/children

corps/corps

economics/economics

Suffixes and Other Word Endings

Several rules tell you how to spell words ending with suffixes. For example, when a one-syllable word ends with one consonant preceded by one vowel (*stop*), double the final consonant (*p*) before adding a suffix that starts with a vowel (*-er*). The same principle applies with a word having a verb ending (*-ed*):

stop/stopper

stop/stopped

When a one-syllable word ends with one consonant preceded by one vowel (*glad*), do *not* double the final consonant (*d*) before adding a suffix that starts with a consonant (*-ly*):

glad/gladly

When a word with more than one syllable ends with one consonant preceded by one vowel (*occur*) and the accent falls on the last syllable, double the final consonant (*r*) before adding a suffix that starts with a vowel (*-ence*). The same principle applies with a word having a verb ending (*-ing*):

occur/occurrence

occur/occurring

When a word with more than one syllable ends with one consonant preceded by one vowel (*differ*) and the accent does not fall on the last syllable, do not double the final consonant (*r*) before adding a suffix that starts with a vowel (*-ence*). The same principle applies with a verb ending (*-ing*):

differ/difference

differ/differing

When a word with one or more than one syllable ends with one consonant preceded by more than one vowel (*appeal*), do not double the final consonant (*l*) before adding any suffix or verb ending:

appeal/appealed

When a word with one or more than one syllable ends with more than one consonant (*hand*), do not double the final consonant (*d*) before adding any suffix:

hand/handful

When a word ends in a silent *e*, drop the *e* before adding a suffix that starts with a vowel (*use/usage*). When a word ends in *ce* or *ge*, keep the *e* before adding a suffix that starts with *a, o,* or *u* (*manage/manage-*

able). When a word ends in a silent *e*, keep the *e* before adding a suffix that starts with a consonant (*manage/management*) unless another vowel precedes the final *e* (*argue/argument*). When a word ends in *ie*, change the *ie* to *y* before adding -*ing* (in most cases, the rule for *ie* words is "*i* before *e* except after *c* or when sounded like *a* as in *neighbor* and *weigh*"):

guide/guidance (drop the *e*)

mile/mileage (an exception)

advantage/advantageous (keep the *e*)

excite/excitement (keep the *e*)

judge/judgment (an exception)

tie/tying (change to *y*)

believe (*i* before *e*)

receive (except after *c*)

science (an exception)

When a word ends in *e* preceded by *c* or *g*, keep the final *e* before adding -*able* or -*ous* but drop the final *e* before adding -*ible*:

manage/manageable

courage/courageous

deduce/deducible

When a word ends in -*ation*, change it to -*able* (other words not ending in -*ation* may also take the -*able* suffix). Otherwise no clear-cut rule exists for determining when to use -*able* or -*ible*:

application/applicable

reputation/reputable

admission/admissible

discern/discernible

Only one word ends in -*sede*: *supersede*. Three words end in -*ceed*: *proceed*, *exceed*, and *succeed*. Otherwise, -*cede* applies:

recede

precede

concede

intercede

Usually when a word has a *c* that sounds like *k* or has a *g* with a hard sound, use *-ance*, *-ancy*, or *-ant*. When a word has a *c* that sounds like *s* or has a *g* with the sound of *j*, use *-ence*, *-ency*, or *-ent*. Otherwise no clear-cut rule exists to determine which suffix to use:

significant

negligent

assistance

intelligence

No rule exists for using *-ize*, *-ise*, and *-yze*. Most words end in *-ize*, very few in *-yze*:

authorize

advertise

analyze

When a word ends in *y* preceded by a consonant, change the *y* to *i* before adding any suffix or verb ending except one beginning with *i* (one-syllable adjectives such as *dry* and certain words such as *ladylike* are exceptions). When a word ends in *y* preceded by a vowel, keep the *y* before adding any suffix or any verb ending:

modify/modified

delay/delayed

dry/drier/dryer/driest/dryly/dryness

secretary/secretaryship

employ/employing

day/daily (an exception)

Prefixes

When a word begins with an *s*, the word formed after adding the prefix *dis-* or *mis-* will have a double *s*:

satisfied/dissatisfied

spell/misspell

appoint/disappoint

applied/misapplied

Troublesome Words

The best way to solve individual problems not covered by any rule is to use your dictionary. Some persons benefit from making a list of troublesome words for quick reference. The following list contains many of the words frequently misspelled in business communication:

absence	amateur
acceptable	amenable
accessible	analysis
accessories	annulment
accidentally	apologize
accommodate	argument
accompanying	assurance
accustom	attendance
achievement	authorize
acknowledge	auxiliary
adequate	believing
adjustment	beneficial
admirable	biannual
advisable	biased
affidavit	bookkeeper
affiliate	buoyant
allotted	bureau
all ready	calendar
all right	canceled
already	cancellation

carburetor

censure

changeable

chargeable

chiefly

clientele

colleague

collectible

commitment

committed

commodities

comparative

competence

competitive

complementary

complimentary

concede

concession

conducive

confer

conference

congratulate

conscientious

consensus

controlled

convenience

correspondence

correspondents

corroborate

council

counsel

courteous

courtesy

creditor

criticism

criticize

deductible

deferred

deficient

deficit

depreciation

desirable

discrepancy

dissatisfied

distributor

embarrass

enforceable

equipped

equitable

equivalent

erroneous

evidently

exaggerate

exceed

exceptionally

exchangeable

existence

exorbitant

extraordinary

familiar

feasible

financial

flexible

forcible

foreign

forfeit

formally

formerly

forty

fulfill

grievance

guarantee

guaranty

harass

hesitancy

hindrance

humorous

hurriedly

illegible

inadequate

inaugurate

incidentally

inconvenience

independent

indispensable

inducement

initiative

insolvency

intelligible

intentionally

intercede

interchangeable

invariable

irrelevant

jeopardize

judgment

justifiable

labeled

laboratory

legible

liable

license

liquidation

livelihood

maintenance

manageable

mediocre

mercantile

merchandise

miniature

miscellaneous

misspell

mortgage

naturally

necessary

negligible

ninety	receivable
ninth	recipient
noticeable	reducible
obsolete	reference
occasionally	referred
offered	regrettable
omitted	remittance
optimistic	retroactive
pamphlet	salable
parliamentary	scarcity
particularly	seize
permissible	serviceable
permitting	siege
perseverance	significance
persistence	specifically
possession	stationary
precedence	stationery
predominant	subsidiary
preferable	substantiate
preference	substitute
preferred	superintendent
prevalent	supersede
procedure	supervisor
proceedings	tendency
profited	traceable
promissory	transferable
proportionate	transferred
questionnaire	traveled
receipt	unanimity

unbelievable	visible
unconscious	warranted
uncontrollable	wholly
unforeseen	witnessed
usage	yield
vicinity	

Professionals apply this general rule to many situations, and it is especially appropriate in matters of spelling: When in doubt, look it up. In addition to general and special-interest dictionaries, other helpful guides are *Sisson's Word and Expression Locater* (Parker Publishing Co.) and *Word Finder* (Prentice-Hall). Since spelling rules don't apply to all cases, you need a combination of aids to correct spelling. A good dictionary is indispensable.

Successful business people know that careless, inaccurate, and inconsistent spelling, punctuation, and capitalization can damage a person's image as an intelligent, well-educated, well-informed, and accomplished professional. All of these many aspects of business writing contribute toward more effective business communication, and better communication means greater success in the modern business world.

4 NONDISCRIMINATORY COMMUNICATION

Discrimination is not always intentional, but the consequences are the same when some word or phrase or the general tone of a business message reflects the subtle or blatant bias of a writer. Sensitive readers will cringe at a writer's indifference to human circumstances. Condescension, stereotypes, ethnic clichés, offensive connotations, patronization, sexism, racism, put-downs, exploitation, demeaning humor—all of these things can be found in today's business communication in spite of equal opportunity laws and practices. Progress is being made, but everyone in the business community needs to reevaluate the depth of his or her sensitivity to human circumstances.

Most people insist that they are sensitive to other people's feelings, but their language suggests otherwise. The aphorism "We are not altogether displeased with the misfortune of others" is unsettling primarily because it is in part true. One could also say, "We are not altogether displeased with the *discomfort* of others." Psychologists remind us how often people try to intensify, not alleviate, someone's discomfort. Think how often you have heard something like this: "Why, Steve, I do believe you're blushing! Hey, everyone—look, quick! Steve is blushing, ho, ho, ho!" Poor old Steve, who was apparently uncomfortable or embarrassed about something, now feels twice as miserable. But he smiles good-naturedly and unquestioningly accepts his friends' insensitivity. He finds it completely natural that they are "not altogether displeased with his discomfort."

As long as people remain thoughtless, indifferent, and uncaring, even among friends, they will have serious problems developing enough genuine sensitivity to overcome discriminatory tendencies at work. Sensitivity is not something you can plug in on certain occasions. It is not good enough to profess equal rights for women at lunch

114

and tell a demeaning ethnic joke at dinner. From a practical stand-point, it's risky to practice part-time sensitivity. Some time when you are off-duty, you may lose a customer or an account or even offend your boss. It is amazing how quickly doors can start closing. But no matter what the motive is, nondiscriminatory communication should be the goal of every business person, and developing a genuine sensitivity toward others with no exceptions is an essential first step.

Eliminating Racial and Ethnic Discrimination

If your organization publishes a newsletter, internal magazine, annual report, or some other publication, examine the photographs in back issues. Look for a photograph that shows a cafeteria, mail room, or stock room. Are the employees shown in the low-level positions black, Mexican-American, or Asian? Compare these scenes with photographs of executives in high-level positions. Are most of the executives white and primarily male? Now examine the language in various pieces of written communication. Do the words and phrases perpetuate negative racial and ethnic attitudes? For example, does the writing mention racial and ethnic groups unnecessarily? Does it imply that blacks, Asians, Mexican-Americans, and so on are always in low-level, serving positions and poor economic circumstances?

Psychology and sociology textbooks usually include discussions of stereotyping, patronizing, and other problems associated with racial and ethnic discrimination. Several books published in the last decade for communicators also treat this subject:

Avoiding Stereotypes (Houghton Mifflin)

Guidelines for Creating Positive Sexual and Racial Images in Educational Materials (Macmillan)

Multi-Ethnic Guidelines (McGraw-Hill)

Racism in the English Language (Racism and Sexism Resource Center in New York)

Random House Guidelines for Multi-Ethnic/Nonsexist Survey (Random House)

Without Bias (International Association of Business Communication in San Francisco)

These and other authorities make clear that the words we use often have negative implications and hence are offensive to certain readers. But habit, insensitivity, inattention to detail, carelessness, haste, and many other influences cause us to use discriminatory language often without even realizing it. Look at these words from an awards presentation speech reprinted in a company newsletter:

> Raymond Jefferson, an outstanding black scientist at. . . .

No one would every say:

> David McKenzie, an outstanding *white* scientist at. . . .

Unless the reference to race is essential to clarify something else, omit it.

Words and the way they are put together can have negative or positive implications. When you use adjectives such as *bright, responsible, industrious, outgoing, quiet, conservative,* and *sophisticated* in conjunction with racial identification, you may be implying that members of a certain racial or ethnic group usually are the opposite:

Remark:	George Stone is a bright, highly responsible black programmer.
Implication:	Blacks are usually not bright and responsible.
Remark:	Kim Chung, an unusually industrious and outgoing member of the advertising staff, is going to prepare the Southwest prospect list.
Implication:	Asians are usually not industrious and outgoing.
Remark:	Marguerite Chavez, a quiet, conservative receptionist in our branch office, has applied for a transfer to our headquarters office.
Implication:	Mexican-Americans are usually not quiet and conservative.
Remark:	Ron "Running Wolf" Burns, a sophisticated new addition to our staff, will handle customer relations in the shipping department.
Implication:	Native North Americans are usually not civilized.

Any comment suggesting that all members of a racial or ethnic group are alike (*stereotyping*) should be taboo. Unfortunately, most stereotypes in business writing are so familiar and obvious that business writers fail to recognize them. The myth persists that:

Blacks are lazy, irresponsible clowns.

Mexican-Americans are hot-tempered, uneducated, and subservient.

Native North Americans are stoic, alcoholic savages.

Asians are cunning, philosophical, and serene.

Anglo-Saxons are conservative, educated, and superior.

Jews are shrewd, enterprising, and rich.

Italians are argumentative, passionate, and manipulative.

Dutch are hardworking, fat, and fanatical about cleanliness.

Many more stereotyped descriptions are used for these and other ethnic and racial groups. The problem is not that business messages boldly state such biases; the problem is that the stereotypes are reinforced by subtle or direct implication. The power of suggestion lurks behind even the most well-intentioned message.

Some business writers divide all people into two groups: white and nonwhite. Can you remember how often you have read about blacks and nonblacks? Most of these writers simply do not understand that people of different heritages are offended by this insistence upon a white reference point for everything:

Poor: The university has changed its admissions policy regarding nonwhite students.

Better: The university has changed its admissions policy regarding students of black, Mexican-American, Asian, and other heritages.

Other words that also seem so common and harmless to many business people in reality humiliate their sensitive readers:

Poor: A new job-training program was established for the disadvantaged minorities.

Better: A new job-training program was established for employees of Asian, black, Mexican-American, and Native North American heritage.

Any policy, attitude, or comment that is patronizing is offensive. Sensitive readers easily detect the condescension of an insensitive writer. Any evidence of tokenism is also unforgivable. Everyone has heard about the token black (or member of some other racial or ethnic group) who is trotted out each week on most white-dominated television programs. The same kind of tokenism can be found in many articles and photographs. Ethnic clichés and trite references are all too familiar as well. One article written for a company house organ was supposed to describe a new energy-efficient pump system. But because the inventor being interviewed had a Chinese heritage, the interviewer couldn't resist inquiring about the subject's abilities in kung fu. In another instance, someone interviewing a black engineer about problems in mineral excavation interjected a question about the subject's favorite soul food. Somehow these incredible things happen.

The risk of offending someone is ever present, and business people who prepare written messages need to be sensitive to any possible negative implications in their writing. Just as you never know whether someone of Asian heritage is standing nearby when you angrily call your competitor yellow (that is, a coward), you never know who may read other unintentional biases in your written messages. Also, as a communicator you are responsible for seeing that your publications conform to affirmative action requirements. Several acts and executive orders (listed in the section "Writing with Respect for the Handicapped") prohibit various forms of job discrimination. You must be certain that your written material cannot be used against your employer by someone bringing a discrimination suit against your organization. If you have any doubts in this area, consult your organization's attorney or write to the Equal Employment Opportunity Commission, 1800 G Street, N.W., Washington, D.C. 20506, for current information.

Writing with Respect for the Handicapped

The most common mistake that business people make in writing to or about the handicapped is that they focus on the handicap instead of the person's abilities. Not only is this offensive, it is unfair. *Disability* is not a synonym for *inability*. A handicapped person may have the ability to perform certain tasks as well as or better than a person without the handicap. Business messages that focus on or sound self-conscious about someone's handicap need to be rewritten, and the writers need to examine their attitudes toward the handicapped.

The people who receive your memos, letters, reports, newsletters, magazine articles, and speeches may have a hearing or speech impairment, epilepsy, blindness, mental illness, paralysis, or any other handicap. But most of these people are active and productive, and they rightfully resent any implication to the contrary. Many words that have been entrenched in the English language for decades have negative, demeaning connotations and should be edited out of all business communication:

Wrong: These steps should be taken if an employee has a fit while at work.

Right: These steps should be taken if an employee has a seizure while at work.

Wrong: Our training classes need to reach employees who are semiretarded.

Right: Our training classes need to reach employees who are slow learners.

Wrong: The design of the cafeteria makes it easy for crippled employees to serve themselves.

Right: The design of the cafeteria makes it easy for disabled employees to serve themselves.

Wrong: Judy Perone, who is deaf and dumb, has joined the staff of our accounting department as an assistant bookkeeper.

Right: Judy Perone, who has a speech and hearing impairment, has joined the staff of our accounting department as an assistant bookkeeper.

Wrong: This report describes new learning devices for the insane.

Right: This report describes new learning devices for the emotionally disturbed.

Most words such as *fit, crippled*, and *insane* are unacceptable in any situation. A few words such as *retarded* may be used in the appropriate context but not as a label for employees who merely learn more slowly than other employees. Some words are controversial. *Mental illness,* for example, is unacceptable to some people; they prefer something such as *emotional difficulties* or *problems in adjustment.* Psychologist Thomas Szasz, for instance, objects strongly to the label *mental illness.* He believes people simply have problems in living. If you are uncertain about some word, you may have to discuss the matter with others in your office, or go directly to your readers and ask what they prefer.

Do not go to the other extreme in your choice of language. Some words may be too blunt and derogatory, but pretending the problem is no more serious than a hangnail is just as offensive. Say that it is your responsibility to write a letter discussing ways to make the working environment more appropriate for someone who uses a wheelchair:

> *Wrong:* I would like to suggest three ways we could set up our laboratory to make it more convenient for you in regard to your little problem.

> *Right:* I would like to suggest three ways we could set up our laboratory to make it more practical for you to use your wheelchair around the test tables.

Just as some business writers stereotype racial and ethnic groups, they also stereotype people with handicaps. Thus you read that all people who cannot walk are exceptionally good at putting things together with their hands, or all people who are blind have extraordinary hearing ability. Applying the attributes of one or a few persons to an entire group is always dangerous and frequently erroneous. It is also a mistake to stereotype by occupation. Retarded persons, for example, do not always load trucks. Unfair stereotyping of handicapped persons is just another form of discrimination.

Some of the rules that apply to racial and ethnic discrimination also apply to discrimination of the handicapped. The writer who made the remark about a black scientist (see the section "Eliminating Racial and Ethnic Discrimination," page 115) would probably make the same type of remark if the scientist were handicapped:

> *Wrong:* Raymond Jefferson, an outstanding deaf scientist at. . . .

> *Right:* Raymond Jefferson, an outstanding scientist at. . . .

The impairment should not be mentioned at all unless it is essential for clarity. Then you might say:

> *Possible:* Raymond Jefferson, who has a hearing impairment, is an outstanding scientist at. . . .

If the impairment must be mentioned, make it incidental:

> *Wrong:* The retarded child is. . . .

> *Right:* The child, who has a learning disability, is. . . .

Wrong: Linda, a deaf employee, is. . . .

Right: Linda, who has a hearing impairment, is. . . .

Do not draw attention to the handicap unless it is essential. If you unquestionably *must* refer to it, at least do not make the person and the handicap inseparable. Do not, for instance, refer to the deaf employee but to the employee who also happens to be deaf:

Not: The mentally ill woman. . . .

But: The woman, who has an emotional problem. . . .

Not: The paraplegic veteran. . . .

But: The veteran, who is a paraplegic. . . .

Not: The epileptic, Joan. . . .

But: Joan, who has epilepsy. . . .

Business people who prepare written communication should follow any changes in equal employment opportunity laws and the affirmative action programs that affect their organizations' employment practices. Your organization's attorney can provide information for you on the Equal Pay Act of 1963, the Civil Rights Act of 1964, the Rehabilitation Act of 1973, and the Vietnam Veterans Readjustment Act of 1974. Various executive orders affect employment opportunities in regard to age, handicap, and veteran status. As a communicator you should keep in mind that your organization's publications could be used to support or defeat any claim of discrimination against your organization.

Discrimination is only one concern when you are writing to or about the handicapped. Your job also may involve educating other employees or the public about the needs and rights of handicapped persons. But no matter what type of message you must prepare, you need to demonstrate a genuine sensitivity for those who have a handicap and beware of discriminatory language that intentionally or unintentionally focuses on disabilities instead of abilities.

Communicating Without Sexual Bias

The question "What do women want?" is heard far less in the 1980s than it was in the 1970s. Smart business people know that any hint of sexual bias in their communication will spotlight their insensitivity and lack of skill in preparing written material. You do not have to be an ardent feminist to understand the importance of writing without sexual bias. However, some business writers are spokespersons for or advocates of a social or political cause. These communicators have special motivations and objectives. But many, perhaps most, business people do not want to appear to be crusading. They prefer to present an image of objectivity. They simply want to handle their writing assignments properly, effectively, and thoughtfully without offending any person or group.

Tradition sometimes seems to be synonomous with stubbornness. Old writing habits are hard to break, and nonsexist writing isn't easy or natural for everyone. Another problem is that some of the rules for communicating without sexual bias are still being written. Business people can expect to see further changes in the next decade, including greater emphasis on existing guidelines. Vocabulary will likely become much more asexual. The titles *Miss* and *Mrs.* may all but disappear from business correspondence being replaced by *Ms.* Both written and visual material will increasingly depict men and women in equal roles, rather than showing women in serving positions. As resistance crumbles, the guidelines given below will become essential ingredients of nondiscriminatory business writing.

Addressing Women

You can solve the problem about which title to use in addressing women simply by using *Ms.* unless you know the woman prefers *Miss* or *Mrs.* In business correspondence *Ms.*, *Miss*, or *Mrs.* precedes a name even when a business title follows it:

Ms. Jacqueline Ryan, Vice-President

Socially you should address a married woman (or a widow) by her husband's full name preceded by *Mrs.* In business you should use either her husband's full name preceded by *Mrs.* or her first name and her married name preceded by *Ms.* or *Mrs.* Some women like to combine both their maiden and married names, often with a hyphen. Use the form of address the woman prefers, if you know it:

Mrs. James Collins (social or business)

Mrs. Arlene Collins (business)

Ms. Arlene Collins (business)

Mrs. Arlene Hyatt-Collins (business)

Ms. Arlene Hyatt-Collins (business)

Socially you should address a divorced woman by her maiden and married names combined preceded by *Mrs.* or by her first name and her maiden name preceded by *Mrs.*, *Miss*, or *Ms.* In business you should use either her first name and her married name preceded by *Mrs.* or *Ms.*; her first name and her maiden and married names combined preceded by *Mrs.*, *Miss*, or *Ms.*; or her first name and her maiden name preceded by *Mrs.*, *Miss*, or *Ms.* The choice of last name for a divorced woman obviously depends on whether she has kept her married name. Use the form the woman prefers, if you know it:

Mrs. Hillyer Canton (social)

Mrs. Donna Hillyer (social or business)

Miss Donna Hillyer (social or business)

Ms. Donna Hillyer (social or business)

Mrs. Donna Canton (business)

Ms. Donna Canton (business)

Mrs. Donna Hillyer-Canton (business)

Miss Donna Hillyer-Canton (business)

Ms. Donna Hillyer-Canton (business)

In business correspondence when you do not know if a person is a man or a woman, do *not* use *Mr.*, as authorities formerly recommended. Simply omit the title:

Dear Leslie Parker:

Dear H. T. McGuire:

When you do not know either name or gender, use one of the following forms:

Dear Madam or Sir:

Dear Sir or Madam:

When an organization includes both men and women, do not use a single-sex greeting:

Not: **Mesdames (or Ladies)**

Not: **Messrs. (or Gentlemen)**

But: **Ladies and Gentlemen:**

Always address professional women by professional titles, if they have them, followed by first name and last name (either maiden or married, whichever the woman prefers). Use the professional title even when the woman's husband is also named:

Dr. Edna Jacobi

Dr. Edna Jacobi and Dr. Peter Jacobi

Drs. Edna and Peter Jacobi

Drs. Peter and Edna Jacobi

Dr. Edna Jacobi and Mr. Peter Jacobi

But always return to this basic rule when you have some doubt: If you do not know a woman's professional title, her marital status, or her preferred form of address, use *Ms.*

Use titles consistently and with equality toward the sexes. Do not refer to Mr. Jenkins and Sally Anne. Either give both or neither person a title (and first or last name):

Wrong:	Edward Towne and Joanne
Right:	Edward Towne and Joanne Kline (or Edward and Joanne)
Wrong:	Mr. Towne and Joanne
Right:	Mr. Towne and Ms. Kline (or Edward and Joanne)
Wrong:	Towne and Joanne
Right:	Towne and Kline (or Edward and Joanne)
Wrong:	Towne and Miss Kline
Right:	Towne and Kline (or Mr. Towne and Miss or Ms. Kline)

Editors like to see full names used in the first instance and last names only (or first names only, if appropriate) thereafter:

Wrong:	Edward Towne and Joanne Kline wrote the new programming manual. Towne and Joanne are also . . .
Right:	Edward Towne and Joanne Kline wrote the new programming manual. Towne and Kline are also. . . .

Sexist references

Learning to write without sexist references may take additional time and effort in the beginning, but this time and effort will be well spent. Many readers are offended by business writing that appears to speak to and about men alone. Skilled business writers substitute asexual words for sexual references:

Sexist:	Mankind still has a lot to learn about international cooperation.
Nonsexist:	People still have a lot to learn about international cooperation.
Sexist:	We devoted over one hundred man-hours to the design and testing functions.
Nonsexist:	We devoted over one hundred hours to the design and testing functions.
Sexist:	The salesmen need to reevaluate their strategy periodically.
Nonsexist:	Sales people need to reevaluate their strategy periodically.
Sexist:	Today's businessmen face greater competition than ever before.
Nonsexist:	Today's business people face greater competition than ever before.

Some language does not specifically include the word *man*, but it nevertheless shows a sexual bias, however subtle the reference might be. Sometimes the bias is far from subtle:

Sexist:	Attending the meeting were Tony Paluzzi, one of our top nuclear engineers, and his attractive assistant Linda Arnold.
Nonsexist:	Attending the meeting were Tony Paluzzi, one of our top nuclear engineers, and his capable assistant Linda Arnold.
Sexist:	The men and the girls from the marketing department attended the annual conference last week.
Nonsexist:	The men and the women (or the staff) from the marketing department attended the annual conference last week.

Sexist:	The woman pilot represented Hartwell's Southern Air Service.
Nonsexist:	The pilot represented Hartwell's Southern Air Service.
Sexist:	You and your wife may select one of three accommodations.
Nonsexist:	You and your spouse may select one of three accommodations.
Sexist:	Each person has to make his own decisions.
Nonsexist:	People must make their own decisions.

As you can see in the above examples, you can frequently eliminate sexism merely by changing a word here and there. Sometimes you may have to weed out descriptions that stereotype, belittle, or trivialize women and their positions. In other situations, you may have to revise the overall tone of your communication to show equal respect for both sexes.

Communicating without sexual bias is especially hard for some business people, not because they do not want to show respect for women, but because they simply do not know how to show it. Others are surprised to learn that women resent the focus on their physical appearance rather than their professional abilities. They wonder why women are not amused by some of the sexual innuendoes and jokes that are part of the daily fare for them. Those who are not yet sensitive to either the blatant or the subtle forms of sexual discrimination in business writing may need more than a few guidelines. Books and articles on this subject are available to help the business communicator write without sexual bias:

Guidelines for Equal Treatment of the Sexes in McGraw-Hill Book Company Publications (McGraw-Hill Book Co.)

Guidelines for Newswriting About Women (Stanford University Women's News Service)

Guidelines for Nonsexist Use of Language in NCTE Publications (National Council of Teachers of English in Urbana, IL)

The International Association of Business Communicators in San Francisco has also dealt with the subject of sexism in its *Journal of Organizational Communication* (Winter 1973) and a 1977 book *Without Bias*. To help you further develop a strong sensitivity to words, images, and other references that concern women, you would benefit from reading some current issues of *Ms.* magazine and the National Organization for Women's *National Now Times*.

The Civil Rights Act of 1964 prohibits discrimination on the basis of race, color, religion, sex, or national origin. Other laws and executive orders (mentioned earlier in this chapter) and your employer's policies also affect your written communication. Whether you are writing a brief interoffice memo or a feature article for a major national magazine, you need to insure that your words are free from even the most subtle, unintentional bias.

As laws and trends in communication change, your writing should reflect each new effort toward equality among all people. Language does not always keep pace with the rapidly, sometimes radically, changing world of business. But genuine sensitivity toward others and a sincere desire to communicate without bias will help to put the rewards of better business writing within reach.

5 EFFECTIVE LETTERS AND MEMOS

Each year business people write more letters and memos than any other type of communication. The millions of these short forms of communication serve a seemingly endless variety of purposes. People get acquainted, introduce products and services, handle transactions, solve problems, build images, and do many other things—all by mail. Most messages either convey information, ask for something, or build goodwill; sometimes a writer combines two or all three objectives in one message. The overall aim is to influence your readers in some way, and the ability to write effective letters and memos is therefore at a premium in the business community.

Most business people have learned (often the hard way) that a well-written message will likely accomplish what a writer wants, but a poorly written message will just as likely fail to accomplish what the writer wants. Clear and forceful correspondence is essential to help you perform successfully at work. Good letters and memos are powerful tools that directly or indirectly can produce billions of dollars in profits for organizations. One of the greatest mistakes a business person can make is to underestimate both the practical value and the critical importance of business correspondence.

No one can truly hide behind a letter or memo. Your messages give your readers a strong and possibly lasting impression of you and the organization you represent. They tell your readers whether you can express yourself intelligently, whether you appear to understand something, whether your thinking is fuzzy or clear, whether you can organize your thoughts logically, whether your are careful or careless with details, whether you are thoughtful or rude, whether you are cold and pompous, and so on. Most letters and memos are far more revealing than a photograph. But if all of the above is true, why are so many

128

messages such a disaster? Why doesn't anyone care enough to do something about this problem of ineffective correspondence? Each situation is different, but a principal reason is that business people simply take letter writing for granted. They don't realize that such a vital link exists between good letter writing and other business activities; that measured in dollars and cents, letters and memos are undeniably a dominant and crucial factor in the conduct of modern business affairs.

Developing an Effective Style and Tone

Readers notice several things in a letter or memo. Does it look attractive? How long is it? Does it sound personal? Does it sound friendly? Is it easy to read? Is the message clear? Is anything missing? Does it have errors in grammar, spelling, and punctuation? Does the opening catch the reader's attention? Does the ending leave the right impression? All of these things together and more make up the style and tone of your message.

Specific examples of an effective writing style are given in chapter 1 in the sections "Learning to Use Active Sentences," "Editing Your Own Writing for Conciseness and Clarity," "Writing Powerful Openers and Effective Endings," "Choosing Precise Words," "Avoiding Cold and Pompous Writing," and "Guarding Against Trite Expressions." Chapter 2 is an alphabetic list of commonly misused words. Chapter 3 gives current rules for spelling, capitalization, and punctuation. Chapter 4 describes words and phrases that indicate racism, sexism, and lack of respect for the handicapped. The introduction "Essentials to Successful Writing" explains four basic steps to follow in preparing written messages, and additional information on organization, research, writing, and editing is given in chapter 6.

Attitude

The world of business is a world of people who need to get along with one another. Basic psychology tells us that the best way to accomplish this is to make the other person feel good. In business correspondence you can do this by adopting what business communicators call the *you* attitude. Many business people may find it difficult to abandon the *I-we* approach, but reader-response tests have shown that the *you* attitude is more effective. Compare these examples and judge for yourself which sound warmer, friendlier, and more concerned with the reader:

We attitude: We believe a strong background in chemistry will help us complete the experimental stage of the project more successfully. Our thanks. . . .

You attitude: Your strong background in chemistry is just what we need to complete the experimental stage of the project more successfully. Thank you. . . .

We attitude: We received your progress report of September 4.

You attitude: Thank you for your progress report of September 4.

I attitude: I find the new transfer features of the BC200 answering machine especially interesting. I would like to receive more information.

You attitude: The new transfer features of your BC200 answering machine are especially interesting. Would you please send more information.

I attitude: I would like to tell you about our 24-hour intercity messenger service.

You attitude: You can now have on-the-spot, personal delivery of your messages anywhere within the city limits by subscribing to our 24-hour messenger service.

The *I-we* versus *you* attitude can be enforced further by taking a positive approach to everthing you say:

Negative: I won't be able to meet with you at 1:30 P.M. on Friday, July 14, but. . . .

Positive: Thanks very much for suggesting a time and date to meet with you. The day, July 14, is fine, but would you be able to change the time to. . . .

Negative: I won't have your information ready until August 11, 19___.

Positive: Your information will be ready August 11, 19___.

A friendly, positive attitude is essential to win friends and influence people, and that is a chief aim of all business communication. Effective business writers use every technique available to them. A conversational tone, with warm and personal references, goes a long way toward winning friends. Notice the difference in tone in these examples:

Poor: Let us know if we can be of further assistance.

Better: If you need more information, Ms. Hendricks, please let us know.

Poor: May I compliment you on your organizational plan. I want to thank you for your contribution.

Better: Your organizational plan looks excellent, Jack. Many thanks for your good work.

The tone of your letter depends on how well you know the reader, but even strangers enjoy a friendly, personal message. Readers may react negatively to cold and unfriendly messages (as described in chapter 1) and may instantly dislike or mistrust the writer. Try to use the reader's name in the body of the letter, as the above examples illustrate, and don't hesitate to use expressions such as *thank you, thanks very much,* and *many thanks.* People feel good when they are appreciated, and in most situations, a chief aim of business communication is to make the other person feel good.

Organization

Letters and memos must look neat and attractive too. Readers see the paper, the letterhead, and the typing before they read the message itself. (The following two sections describe basic formats and the standard parts of letters and memos, explaining where and how they should be positioned on a page. The final section of this chapter shows actual examples of different types of letters and memos for different occasions.) Length also affects the appearance of a message and its readability. Skilled writers strive for conciseness (see the section on this subject in chapter 1) and strictly observe this rule: Keep it short and keep it simple.

Developing the message (getting thoughts in proper sequence leading to the desired conclusion) is difficult for many people. (The Introduction offers some valuable and *practical* tips for writers who have trouble collecting their thoughts logically on paper.) The opening should always briefly state the purpose of the letter and set the stage for what follows. If it doesn't attract the reader immediately, the impact of the entire message may be lost. The reader must be encouraged to go on to the body of the letter, where information should be stated in a logical sequence. If action is required of the reader, the message should state a specific date (*not* "as soon as possible"). Immediately after all necessary information is presented, the message should conclude with one or two sentences that leave the reader with the desired impression. Remember the professional's golden rule: Keep it short and keep it simple. The final section of this chapter shows the actual development of letters and memos. Here are examples of ways to make openings more effective:

> *Poor:*   I would like to introduce a system we developed to process back orders more efficiently and at lower cost.

> *Better:*   If processing back orders is costing you precious time and money, an easy, inexpensive solution may be only as far away as your mailbox.

> *Poor:*   Replying to your letter of November 14, 19____, we wish to inform you that the booklet you requested is currently out of stock.

> *Better:*   Thank you for letting us know about your interest in "Ten Ways to Save Money in the Supermarket." A new supply of this booklet will soon be available, and your copy will be sent promptly on December 1.

A good opening should arouse the interest of your reader, indicate why you are writing or what you are writing about, direct the reader into the body of the letter, and set a friendly, thoughtful tone for the overall message. Both openings and endings should be short; these are not the places to carry on a long-winded monologue. Here are some examples of final paragraphs that bring things to an appropriate close without needless repetition and discussion:

> Why not sign and mail the enclosed card today? A copy of *Lifeline Reports* will be on your desk next week.

> Many thanks for your help and patience, Judy. It was a joy to work with you.

> May I call on you next Friday, August 7, at 2:30 P.M.? You can reach me in my office weekdays at 555-7400 and at home evenings and weekends at 555-2211.

> Don't wait! The sooner you begin, the sooner you will be on the way to that big promotion you've always wanted.

To save you time, Bill, a duplicate copy of this letter is enclosed. Just initial the proposed clause and return the letter to me. I'll take it from there.

The closing should let readers know what they must do (if anything) and when (if a deadline is involved). The objective of the letter determines the type of closing. Credit letters about long overdue accounts would try to jolt readers into responding with their payments. But sales letters to prospective customers would try to entice, not pressure, readers. Each situation is different, and common sense is usually the best guide in choosing the appropriate tone and emphasis.

Selecting a Basic Format

Many offices have a standard letter or memo format used by all employees. The four commonly used business styles are the full-block, block, modified-block, and simplified formats. Most business letters are typed on 8½- by 11-inch stationery (personal letters are sometimes typed on executive letterhead, 7¼ by 10½ inches). Memo formats and paper sizes vary widely, although most include basic guide words (*Date, To, From,* and *Subject*) at the head of the page. An explanation of the format is given in each sample letter shown in the next section.

Preparing the Standard Parts of Letters and Memos

Composing your letter or memo is the most difficult part of preparing business correspondence. It may be the only part that concerns you. But your readers will notice more than that. In almost all types of business writing, appearances matter a great deal. Your message may be brilliant, but if your letters and memos do not use and position the principal elements properly, your readers will not be favorably impressed with your skill as a communicator. Each of the standard parts of letters and memos are described below alphabetically. Examples of many of these elements appear in the letter formats illustrated on pages 134–38.

Attention Line

When a letter is addressed to a firm, you can direct it to a particular department or person by using an attention line (Attention Data Processing Department; Attention Ms. Ellen Schotts). If that person is absent, someone else in the firm or department will handle the matter.

January 9, 19____

CONFIDENTIAL

Ms. Marcia Perone
ABC Secretarial Services
17 Nassau Street
Princeton, NJ 08540

Dear Ms. Perone:

Subject: Full-Block Format

This is an example of the full-block format. The clean, fresh look is preferred in many modern business offices.

All principal parts of the letter are typed flush left, with two line spaces between paragraphs and most principal parts of the letter. The subject line is positioned immediately below the salutation.

The full-block format is especially popular as a time-saver. Since everything is blocked against the left margin, typists do not have to set up and use tabulator stops.

Sincerely,

David R. Winslow
Office Manager

cl

Enc.

cc: M. T. Burns

Full-Block Format

(LETTERHEAD)

January 9, 19____

Our File 77ID

Modern Stationers
P.O. Box 1700
Brisbane, CA 94005

Attention Mr. Herman Bellows

Gentlemen:

This is an example of the block format. It differs from the full-block style in that not all parts of the letter are positioned flush left.

The dateline and the reference line are typed against the right margin. The complimentary close and signature lines are positioned at center page or just to the right of center page. All other elements are typed flush left.

Many companies choose the block format because it too is easy to set up, looks modern and attractive, and is slightly less extreme than the full-block format.

Sincerely,

Janet Minelli
Business Manager

aj

P.S. If you would like additional information about the mechanics of business letters, please let me know.

Block Format

(LETTERHEAD)

January 9, 19____

Your Reference 00711

Ms. Catherine Roberts
Jones & Hardy, Inc.
115 Miller Avenue
Peoria, IL 61615

Dear Ms. Roberts

    Subject: Modified-Block Format

    This is an example of the modified-block format. Unlike the full-block or block formats, paragraphs are indented with this style.

    As with the block style, the dateline and reference line are typed against the right margin. The complimentary close and signature lines are positioned at center page or just to the right of center page. Notice that the subject line and postscript are indented like each paragraph.

    The modified-block format has always been a favorite among traditionalists and, in spite of a trend toward a modern look in letters, will likely remain a favorite in many offices for years to come.

                            Sincerely,

                            Alvin O. Weiman
                            Corresponding Secretary

ar

    P.S. Let me know if I can send you any further information.

Modified Block Format

(LETTERHEAD)

January 9, 19____

Mr. Ralph Kurzig
M & M Educational Services
200 Center Street, N.W.
Washington, DC 20003

SIMPLIFIED FORMAT

This is an example of the simplified format, Mr. Kurzig.
Although some firms believe it is less personal than the other
styles, its modern, easy-to-type format appeals to an increasing
number of busy executives and their secretaries.

The most obvious deviation from the other styles is the
omission of a salutation and complimentary close. Otherwise, it
resembles the full-block format. Notice that the subject line is
typed in capital letters without the word subject. The signature
is also typed in capital letters all in one line.

Advocates of this format, Mr. Kurzig, attempt to overcome any
suggestion that the style is impersonal by using the reader's
name in the opening and closing paragraphs.

SONIA EMOD, DIRECTOR OF BUSINESS SERVICES

sk

Simplified Format

To: Alexander Ratcliff   From: John Stern

Subject: Memo Format   Date: January 9,

Memos were once thought of strictly as interoffice communications. Now many executives with a heavy work load use the memo more and more to correspond with colleagues and others outside the office. Some employees like to use the memo to place orders or make requests, in the absence of a company purchase order form.

Formats vary from preprinted multiple-form sets and various speed-message pads to company-designed memo letterheads. Most forms contain several guide words (To, From, Subject, Date) positioned at the top of the page. Some include a signature line at the bottom of the sheet. Paragraphs are usually typed flush left. The salutation and signature line are usually omitted, although the writer's initials are often typed or signed at the conclusion of the left paragraph.

Miscellaneous notations are positioned below the memo just as they would be in a letter.

JS

an

cc: Darlene Sekowsky

Memo Format

The attention line is positioned directly below the inside address. Each major word is capitalized, but the trend is away from underscoring.

Body

The body of a letter usually starts after the salutation or subject line (if one is used). In the simplified format, the body begins after the inside address or subject line. Paragraphs are indented or typed flush left depending upon the style selected (see the sample letter formats in the preceding section).

Carbon-Copy Notation

When you send a carbon copy to someone other than the addressee, make a notation (cc: Mrs. Dana Camora) beneath the last item of the letter. If you don't want the addressee to know you are sending a copy elsewhere, add a blind-copy notation (bcc: Mrs. Dana Camora) in the upper left corner only on that particular carbon copy and on your file copy.

Complimentary Close

The trend is toward an informal, personal complimentary close: *Sincerely, Cordially, Best regards, Best wishes.* Formal closings such as *Yours very truly* and *Respectfully yours* are seldom used except in legal and official correspondence. The complimentary close is typed below the body of the letter in most of the standard formats, but it is omitted in the simplified letter format. Never precede the closing with the old-fashioned phrase *I remain* (*not* "With all good wishes, I remain" or "Thanking you in advance, I remain").

Continuation Pages

Do not use the word *continued* or *cont.* at the bottom of a page that will run over. On additional pages of a letter, use a heading at the top that includes the addressee's name, the date, and the page number (Michael Owens   -2-   August 5, 19____).

Dateline

Traditionally datelines are typed at the top of the page: month, day, and year (December 14, 19____). But some organizations, particularly the military, put the day first (14 December 19____) with no commas.

Enclosure Notation

Several styles are used to indicate that you are sending something with your letter: *Enclosure; Enc.; 2 Enc.; Enc. 2; Enclosures 2; Enclosures: Check, Invoice.* This notation is positioned beneath the reference initials. Use the words *Separate cover* if the item is being sent separately; *Separate cover 2; Under separate cover: Brochure, Price List.* This notation is positioned beneath the enclosure notation (if any) or the reference initials.

Inside Address

Include the name of the person (or at least a title such as *Sales Manager*), the name of the organization, the street address or post office box, and the city, state, and zip code. Omit the addressee's job title if it makes the address run over four lines. Postal authorities ask everyone to use the two-letter state abbreviations listed on page 100. Be certain the inside address and the address on the envelope are the same.

Mail Notation

Special Delivery, Registered, and other mail notations are typed above the inside address on carbon copies only. The same notation is typed in capital letters on the envelope in the upper right corner just beneath the postage.

Personal or Confidential Notation

Type the word *Personal* or *Confidential,* in all-capital letters or with an initial capital and underscored, beneath the dateline against the left margin. Type the same notation on the envelope beneath the return address.

Postscript

Type comments unrelated to the message of your letter beneath the last notation on the letter, using the initials *P.S.* Put the sender's initials immediately after the postscript message.

Reference Initials

The initials of the typist (rt) are positioned at the left margin beneath the signature lines. If the sender's name is not given in the signature line, put his or her initials before those of the typist (JM:rt).

Reference Line

Some organizations have the words *In reply, please refer to* printed on their letterhead. Put your file number, code number or other reference information after this line: *In reply, please refer to: MMI-Z*. When you reply to a letter with such a number, position a responding notation under your dateline: *Your reference: MMI-Z*.

Salutation

All letter formats except the simplified format include a salutation. The trend is toward an informal greeting: *Dear Helen, Dear Roy, Dear Mrs. Melville, Dear Friends*. Formal greetings such as *Sir* or *My dear Mr. Ortega* are reserved for official correspondence. The section "Communicating Without Sexual Bias," page 121, discusses some special problems in addressing women.

Signature

Signature lines for individuals may have a person's name alone or the name plus job title or the name, job title, and department (everything is in capital letters in the simplified letter format):

Richard Parrish

Richard Parrish
Manager

RICHARD PARRISH — MANAGER

Richard Parrish, Manager
Purchasing Department

Professional persons who want to be addressed in a specific way should type the appropriate title after their names (Michelle Donnovan, M.D.). Women may put *Mrs.* or *Miss* in parentheses before their name: *(Miss) Jennifer Cross*. If no title is indicated readers should assume that the woman prefers to be addressed as *Ms*. Company names are usually typed in capital letters as follows:

Sincerely yours,

COLE INDUSTRIES

Jonathan P. Shurter
Budget Director

Subject Line

Many writers put the subject line after the inside address in all letter formats. The correct position is after the inside address in the simplified format and after the salutation in all other formats. Capitalize each major word: *Subject: Letter Writing in a Nutshell*. The trend is away from underscoring.

Memos may include some of the same parts as a letter handled in the same way: carbon-copy notation, reference initials, enclosure notation, and continuation heading for additional pages. But the memo has no inside address, salutation, attention line, or complimentary close. Often it has no signature line, only the initials of the writer. The body is usually typed in a block format the same as for full-block and block format. The heading of a memo usually includes the guide words *Date, To, From,* and *Subject* (see the sample in the preceding section). No firm rule exists, and an organization may design its own format with its own guide words. Some firms, for instance, might want the heading to include a reference notation line or a line for the name of the addressee's department. Memos are meant to provide a means for rapid, easy communication, and different styles may be designed for different types of organization.

Using Sample Letters and Memos for Different Occasions

After mastering the rules about and techniques for style, tone, grammar, spelling, and punctuation, the time comes when you must put it all together and compose the perfect letter or memo. Chances are you will settle for an almost-perfect, clear, and forceful message. It always helps to have some models to look at, and this section offers sample letters and memos concerning the most common areas of business activity: acknowledgments, appointments, appreciation and goodwill, complaints and adjustments, credit and collection, follow-up and reminders, introductions and references, requests and inquiries, reservations and orders, sales promotion, and social-business letters and invitations.

Acknowledgments

Thoughtful business people respond promptly to messages and material they receive. Often these letters are brief, stating what is received and expressing appreciation for it. Sometimes additional material or information is sent along with the acknowledgment.

Dear Mr. Aldrich:

Thanks very much, Mr. Aldrich, for sending us your detailed proposal to promote next year's Performing Arts Series. Your preliminary suggestions are interesting, and our executive committee would like to learn more about your ideas.

Could you meet with us Thursday, October 13, at 3:00 P.M., and make a full presentation to the committee? An outline is enclosed showing the type of detailed information the committee needs to make a decision. If you have samples from previous campaigns to include in your presentation, it would help the committee visualize the package you have in mind.

Please write or telephone me by Tuesday, October 11, to let me know if you will be able to make a presentation on Thursday. I hope you can. We all appreciate your interest in our Performing Arts Series.

Sincerely,

Appointments

Plans are constantly being made for large and small conferences, interviews, and other meetings. Frequently arrangements are made and confirmed by telephone, but many appointments are confirmed by memo or letter (communication experts say that all but the most casual appointments should be confirmed in writing). Letters making or confirming appointments should always suggest or repeat the time, place, and date.

TO: M. R. Esmond

FROM: D. S. Simon

SUBJECT: Luncheon Appointment

Miles, I'm sorry to let you know that an unexpected
complication in my schedule will prevent me from meeting you
for lunch on Tuesday, August 4. Would Wednesday, August 5, at
12:30, be convenient for you?

If Wednesday is just as satisfactory, could you have your
secretary phone my office to let me know? As soon as I
hear, I'll make new reservations for us at the Sea Lion
Restaurant.

Thanks very much, Miles. I'm looking forward to seeing you
soon.

                                                DSS

Appreciation and Goodwill

Letters that favorably influence the feelings and attitudes of others
are vital assets to an organization. Messages of appreciation and goodwill should therefore be a significant part of every business person's
correspondence. The mistake many people make in this type of letter is
sounding too effusive to be genuine. The expression must always
sound natural and sincere.

Dear Mr. Watson:

Thank you so much for arranging such an interesting and
educational tour of your new research center. Your scientists
and engineers worked hard to help me understand the center's
changing needs and objectives.

The service you provide not only to the aerospace industry
but to the nation is critical to the welfare of all citizens
everywhere. Knowing this, it's a great pleasure for us to
provide the backup equipment in your control complex.

I sincerely appreciated your time and thoughtful attention,

Mr. Watson, and do hope you and your staff will be able to visit our facilities in Milwaukee next month.

Best regards,

Complaints and Adjustments

Everyone makes mistakes, and eventually most business people have to complain about or apologize for something. Complaints require firmness, but unreasonable anger rarely serves any useful purpose. Adjustments should be handled promptly, with consideration and honesty; the best policy if you are wrong is to admit it and apologize.

Dear Mrs. Blakely:

We were indeed sorry to learn that your order for twenty-four programming manuals arrived after your data-processing class had begun. Unfortunately, our company does not offer a discount under such circumstances.

However, if the manuals have not been used, you may return them for a full refund or credit on a future order. If you decide to return the manuals, please send them to the attention of our Order Department and specify whether a credit or refund is desired.

We sincerely regret the inconvenience you have experienced and will do our utmost to see that future orders are filled to your satisfaction.

Cordially,

Credit and Collection

In our credit society, matters of credit and collection are big business. Honesty, accuracy, and respect for a firm's or an individual's privacy are essential. Credit information is often sent on a form, but smaller firms may request or send credit information by letter. Collections are a specialty and usually involve a series of requests for payment. The model shown here is an example of the last in a series of previous, more conciliatory attempts to collect and overdue account.

Dear Mr. Feffer:

We tried. But since you did not reply to our letter of April 1, I regret that we must take other action to collect the balance of your past-due account of $791.40.

If your check for the full amount does not reach us by May 1, you will next hear from the Barton Collection Agency. Please act now and avoid the further damage to your credit standing and possible costs you may incur if legal action is necessary.

Send us your check for $791.40 by May 1, and the matter will be resolved before the Barton Collection Agency takes other action.

Sincerely,

Follow-up and Reminders

People who fail to acknowledge appointments or deadlines leave you wondering almost to the last minute whether they are going to do what you asked them to do. Unfortunately, this happens a lot of the time, and follow-up letters and other reminders are necessary. Tactful business people do not accuse others of being thoughtless or forgetful. They merely repeat the facts of the original commitment or request and hope that the recipient will respond this time.

TO: Ms. Bernbach, Shipping Department

FROM: F. R. Whitehall, Purchasing Department

SUBJECT: Our Order SO-948

On June 27 I placed a rush order for two boxes (ten each) of your 60-minute magnetic cassettes, item no. 12-8282, mfg. no. 20080. Since the cassettes have not arrived, my original order may have been lost; if so, please consider this a duplicate.

We are urgently in need of these cassettes, and I would appreciate having our order sent immediately by UPS to my attention at our letterhead address. If the cassettes are not available, please phone me right away at 555-2020.

Thank you.

FRW

Introductions and References

Letters of introduction or recommendation discuss personal and professional characteristics. Usually they mean a great deal to the subject of the letter and should be composed with a unique blend of diplomacy and honesty. Requests for a reference or introduction should show appreciation. These letters are troublesome to write for many persons. Some writers feel compelled to praise a subject unrealistically. Sometimes letters of introduction sound pushy and demanding, when they should be giving the recipient an opportunity to refuse the proposed meeting. Since letters of introduction and reference are sensitive, they must be written with great care and consideration for both the subject and the recipient.

Dear Mr. Bazinet:

It's a pleasure to introduce Ms. Robin Spier to you as a possible candidate for a position in your art department. She will be calling you next week to request an interview.

Ms. Spier, formerly assistant art director at Artech Advertising Consultants in New York City, is seeking employment in the Los Angeles area, where she has been working on a free-lance basis since moving here last July. Artech has handled several of our campaigns, so I am familiar with Ms. Spier's considerable talent, ingenuity, and professionalism. In addition, she is a thoroughly delightful person to know and approaches each task with dedication and a strong sense of responsibility.

I'd appreciate any consideration you can extend to her, and if I can offer additional information, just let me know. Thanks very much, Mr. Bazinet.

Sincerely,

Requests and Inquiries

Letters asking for something or replying to some request are among the most common of all forms of business correspondence. It surprises many people to learn that such routine messages are often poorly written. Many fail to be explicit about what is wanted. Some are unnecessarily cold and abrupt. Others neglect even to express basic appreciation for some favor or special effort. Also, in the world of business, one often has to say no to some request; in those cases, it never hurts to say no nicely.

Dear Sylvia:

Thanks very much for letting us see your plans for extending the left wing of our Seaton Hall dormitory. You obviously share the concern we all have about overcrowding, and we sincerely appreciate the serious attention you've given to this problem.

The board of trustees has been negotiating to purchase adjacent land on our western property line. If the negotiations are successful, the prospect of a new dormitory may become a reality. The board would then likely postpone any consideration of a new wing for Seaton Hall for several years. Because of this turn of events, an immediate decision concerning your plans does not appear probable; nevertheless, your concept is well founded, and we would like to keep it available for possible future action.

Everyone on the board wants you to know how much we value your concern and efforts on our behalf. Don't be surprised if we call on you later, Sylvia.

Many thanks.

Cordially,

Reservations and Orders

You may place some orders and reservations on special forms (purchase order or requisition). Or you may place them by telephone and follow up with a letter or form. Or you may simply write a memo or letter. In any case, ordering something is part of the daily fare in business, and the key word is *accuracy*. The right information and enough information is essential to insure that your request is filled properly and on time.

TO: Shipping Department
      Office Supplies, Inc.

FROM: J. J. Attle
        Purchasing Department

SUBJECT: ORDER NO. 112

Please send us the following items to be billed to Mobile Architectural Services, Inc., 2020 Washington Street, Dedham, MA 02026:

    One (1) item 46-1804, Matrix Slide Retrieval/Storage Cabinet, $265.00.

    One (1) item 48-0161, Matrix Attaché Viewer, $216.00.

    One (1) item 49-7250, Matrix Slide Editing Retrieval Overlay, $28.00.

Please send these items to the attention of William Oberman, Director, at Mobile Architectural Services, Inc. Thank you.

JJA

Sales Promotion

Sales letters may be part of a large campaign or individual efforts to promote some product or service. Letters that are part of a campaign typically are written as a series of messages to prospective buyers, often addressed "Dear Friend," "Dear Reader," or "Dear Customer." The individual letter may simply represent an unexpected opportunity to arouse interest in some product or service. In one sense, every letter is a sales letter whether it is promoting an idea, a product, or merely goodwill. One of the most important aspects of writing sales promotion letters is reader analysis. Writers should always understand their readers, but sales letters in particular are designed to produce a direct monetary return. Failure to judge the readers' interests and desires may mean failure to produce income.

Dear Friend:

Would you like to give your home a touch of luxury from days gone by—an authentic replica of the famous New England Weather House that once graced the houses of our nation's prominent founders?

Since you may not have as large a household staff as some of our famous founders, we've had this beautiful 12-inch, handmade replica fully antiqued so it will never need polishing. Its gracious lustre will last throughout the years, and its miniature pilgrim forecasters, who stroll out to tell you about a change in the weather, will delight your guests.

You might expect to pay dearly for such a meticulous, 100 percent, handcrafted treasure. But if you act now, you can still obtain this decorator's gem for only $19.99. Our supply is limited, and we must receive your order by midnight, August 31, 19____ , to assure delivery at this special, low price.

Use the enclosed coupon to order your authentic New England Weather House art treasure today. Tomorrow you'll be glad you did.

Cordially,

Social-Business Letters and Invitations

Many social occasions involve business associates, and many occasions combine social and business activities: luncheons, dinners, dances, parties, weddings, anniversaries, birthdays, funerals. Social-business letters and invitations usually have a slightly different tone from strictly business messages. Often it is inappropriate even to hint of business matters in a social-business situation. These letters should have a strong personal touch with clear evidence of naturalness and sincerity.

Dear Employee:

The board of directors of Hillside Plastics, Inc., cordially

invites you and your guest to a winter carnival at the
Springfield Convention Center on Friday evening, December 21.

Our winter carnival will open with cocktails and snacks at
7:30 P.M. in the Snowbird Lounge. Free tickets will be provided
for all employees and guests who want to attend the ice show
at the center from 8:30 to 9:30 P.M. Those who do not attend
the show are invited to stay with us for an evening of music
and dancing in the Snowbird Lounge.

We sincerely hope you and your guest can join us Friday
evening. Please send your reply to Margaret Hochmann in the
Personnel Department by December 12.

Cordially,

6 BUSINESS REPORTS AND ARTICLES

Romanticists may insist that love makes the world go round, but business analysts are more likely to argue that business communication makes the business world go round. Forms of business communication such as reports and articles come in all sizes and shapes. They may be formal or informal and may range from a one-page memo to a several-hundred-page book. They may be one-time or periodic efforts prepared for superiors, other co-workers, customers, prospective customers, special-interest groups, or the general public. They may be written to inform, sell, persuade, debate, or fill some other need. Business reports, articles, proposals, publicity releases—all of such forms of communication are researched and written specifically to give readers the information they need to form an opinion, make a decision, or take some action.

Many business people are involved in all or most of the familiar reporting situations. Some organizations have standard formats that employees use to submit weekly, monthly, or quarterly reports. Proposals are often written informally, with no particular format, when a superior simply asks for "ideas" on how to handle something. The circumstances vary so widely that no single style or format can be used for every report, proposal, article, and publicity release. But each of these forms of communication involves organization, research, drafting, and revision (as explained in the Introduction, "Essentials of Successful Writing"). The ability to prepare effective, readable reports, articles, and similar communication is essential for you to advance in the modern working world. Successful business communication is the backbone of a successful business career.

Determining the Types of Report and Article Writing

How can you determine the most appropriate format and style for each situation? Sometimes the decision will be immediately obvious and sometimes you can easily find out how certain information is usually prepared in your office. Or you may have to analyze what you want to accomplish and which avenues are open to you, selecting the best one or best combination of communication forms.

Business Reports

Probably the format you will most often be called on to use in your career is the business report, short and informal or long and formal. Short, informal reports are commonly prepared on memo stationery. Such reports follow the memo format described in chapter 5. You would not use preliminary pages (such as a title page and table of contents) or end matter (such as an appendix and a bibliography) in a short memo report. You might attach some supplementay material to the memo (such as a chart, table, budget, or pamphlet). You might also use article- and report-style subheads in the memo body to organize your material for clarity and readability:

TO: D. M. Reston

FROM: L. L. Winters

SUBJECT: Status Report—Internal Reorganization

ORGANIZATION: The attached organization chart shows the new functional configuration we have adopted. Reporting to the general manager are the controller, merchandise manager, publicity manager, and store manager. All other predominant functional positions have been grouped under the appropriate level of authority.

STAFF RESPONSIBILITIES: All advisory and supplemental duties—formulating policy proposals, planning programs, periodically reviewing and appraising operations, and consulting with and servicing line executives—have been assigned to staff members.

IMPLEMENTATION: New offices have been established and employees have started working on new assignments.

BUDGET: A revised reorganization budget is attached. Effective January 1, 19____ , reorganization expenses exceeded original estimates by 12 percent. The increase occurred in materials costs for changing office layouts.

STATUS: Reorganization will be completed January 31, 19____ , and all stations will be fully operational by February 15, 19____ .

LLW

Both formal and informal reports are usually prepared on 8½- by 11-inch paper. A large, formal report may be typeset and bound in a separate cover. A small, less formal report may have a title page, typed on the same paper as the rest of the report, and following the title page, a table of contents (see the illustrations in this section). Some writers put an abstract (a one-page summary of the findings, conclusions, and recommendations written in paragraph or list style) after the table of contents. If a letter of transmittal does not accompany the report, writers usually include a foreword (a one-page commentary that indicates why the report was written, for whom, its scope, and any special features that help "sell" it to the readers or arouse interest in it) before the table of contents.

The body of the report should follow the outline you develop to do your research (see the section "Organizing the Topics," page 166, and the introduction to this book, "Essentials of Successful Writing"). If you include tables and charts (see the section "Handling Tables and Charts," page 173), position them at appropriate places in the text or collect them all at the end in an appendix. Be certain to mention each one in the body of the report so the readers will understand the relation of each one to a particular place in your discussion. A formal report, and many informal reports, should have a bibliography at the end. If you put each source you consult on a 3- by 5-inch card during the research stage, it will be easy to alphabetize the cards later and type from them as you prepare the bibliography. Use this style:

DeVries, Mary A. Guide to Better Business Writing.
    Piscataway, N.J.: New Century Publishers, 1981.
Blazek, Mark C. "Grammar Grappler." Writer's Digest,
    September 1979.

Before you type the final copy of the bibliography, edit and revise your rough drafts as explained in the introduction, "Essentials of Successful Writing," and in the section "Writing and Editing." If you are

MANAGEMENT OF TIME

James B. Snowden
Wyatt & Hill Consultants
Denver, Colorado

August 20, 19____

Title Page.   An informal report usually identifies the writer
at the bottom of the title page. A more formal report would
also indicate, under the title, for whom the report is
prepared.

CONTENTS

Foreword ii

Abstract iv

Time Awareness 1

    Reducing Work Loads 3

    Analyzing Time Expenditures 7

    Using a Time Checklist 9

Time Priorities 11

    Budgeting Time 12

    Doing Two Things at Once 16

    Using Timesaving Techniques and Devices 19

    Applying the Output Principle 21

Summary and Conclusions 26

Recommendations 28

Appendix 30

Bibliography 35

Table of Contents. List your major subheads in the table of contents with page numbers. A short, informal report might have only a few subheads and no foreword, abstract, summary and conclusions, recommendations, appendix, or bibliography.

typing the final copy for typesetting, following the suggestions in the last section of this chapter, "Arranging for Printing and Production."

Articles

Business people use articles to address a wider audience than they might reach in a report. Having an article published in a magazine or journal has numerous benefits. The author establishes himself or herself as an authority, gaining new respect and recognition at the same time. To most people, having something published is a worthwhile achievement that can only enhance their careers and their stature among colleagues and co-workers.

Each publication has its own readership and its own requirements for content, length, approach, style, and tone. With articles, it is a serious mistake to follow vague, general rules or guidelines without first studying back issues of the selected periodical. Professional writers carry this advice one step further. Not only do they study articles that have already appeared in the periodical, they query the appropriate editor to determine whether the magazine or journal is even interested in the article idea. After all, why spend a lot of time researching and writing an article only to receive a note from an editor saying, "Sorry, we just purchased a piece on this same subject."

Make your query tantalizing. Open your letter with an interesting fact or question to let the editor know you have something new and fresh and important to offer the publication's readership. For example:

> Fast-buck artists offer "get-rich-quick" and "earn-big-money-in-your-spare-time" gimmicks every day—but so do some honest and legitimate concerns. Yet consumers lose millions of dollars from illegal advertising each year. How can consumers tell a gimmick from a genuine opportunity? Mailing and advertising experts say that the public can use several techniques to distinguish a rip-off from an honest offer.
>
> Would your magazine be interested in a 1,500-word article exposing this national scandal and explaining ways to avoid becoming a victim?

Be certain to enclose a stamped, self-addressed envelope with your query letter. Once you have a green light, organize your project (as described in the introduction to this book) to meet the editor's requirements and the deadline for submitting your manuscript. After you have researched your project thoroughly and have revised your

rough drafts as often as necessary, type the final manuscript copy double-spaced on 8½- by 11-inch paper.

Proposals

Some proposals are requested; others you may write without a
specific request. Of course, it helps if you receive a request for the
proposal; that means someone already recognizes the need for your
idea, and you don't have to start from scratch and convince someone
about its merits.

With some solicited proposals, you will be given a preprinted
form, and your task will be to fill in the blanks. Or you may be in-
structed to prepare a few paragraphs under certain headings such as
abstract, introduction, methodology, management, staff, budget, conclusions, appendix, and bibliography. Such a plan of organization and
breakdown of topics closely resembles a formal business report.

Even if you are preparing an unsolicited proposal, you may want
to organize the topics in a similar way. A brief, informal proposal
might be prepared in the memo proposal format (see the illustration on
page 159), with supplementary material, such as a budget, attached
to the memo. A more formal, solicited proposal would likely have a
special cover sheet provided by the person making the request. An
unsolicited, less formal proposal might have a cover page similar to the
title page of a business report.

Proposals, even solicited ones, must be well written and persua-
sive. Most of them involve money, perhaps large sums of money. It
would be unreasonable to expect someone to release funds unless your
proposal demonstrates your ability to do what needs to be done and to
do it better than anyone else. You need to keep in mind that you are
expected, legally, to do what you propose to do, if your proposal is
accepted and funds are released for that purpose. In several ways proposals are a demanding test of your ability to write honestly, accurately, and persuasively.

Publicity Releases

Organizations that send a lot of releases to the media usually have
8½- by 11-inch news release letterhead paper. Otherwise, writers use
company letterhead. Either way, a standard format must be followed
to minimize the amount of work an editor has to do to make the item
publishable. The more newsworthy an item is, and the less a busy
editor has to do to it, the better the chances are that it will be published.

(MEMO LETTERHEAD)

DATE:

TO:

FROM:

SUBJECT:

INTRODUCTION

_____

_____

_____

METHODOLOGY

_____

_____

_____

MANAGEMENT

_____

_____

_____

STAFF

_____

_____

_____

BUDGET

_____

_____

_____

CONCLUSIONS

_____

_____

_____

                        _____

                                Signature

Enc.

_____

Memo Proposal Format

At the upper right of the page, indicate when the information may be released:

FOR IMMEDIATE RELEASE

FOR RELEASE Monday, June 7, 19____ , 12:00 Noon

Begin the first paragraph with a dateline for out-of-town releases:

Dayton, Ohio (July 13). _____

_____

_____

Some authorities recommend adding a headline centered above the text; others advise against it. In any case, it is not required or essential.

Double-space all copy. At the bottom of the first of two or more pages, center the word MORE. At the end of the last page, center the symbol -30-. Do not split paragraphs at the end of a page, and leave adequate margins on all sides for the editor to mark instructions for the compositor. (See the sample format on page 162.)

Releases are meant to be accurate and well written but not beautiful. Mimeographed copies are fine. The text itself should be carefully edited. Releases must be factual *news* items. Thus adjectives such as *tremendous* and *fabulous*, which you might use in an advertisement, are out of place in the news release. Some of the suggestions in chapter 1 are especially pertinent to news release writing; in particular, notice the example of clichés in the section "Editing Your Own Writing for Conciseness and Clarity." Many business writers benefit from studying news items already published in periodicals. Such items show how periodicals use the information—appropriate content, how long each bulletin is, style of writing, and so forth.

Learning Where and How to Do Research

Research is the basis of decision making. Business people depend on accurate information to complete their assignments, and fact finding in a business office is as common as answering the telephone. Reports, articles, proposals, publicity releases, and other reporting forms use a collection of organized facts taken from a variety of sources: personal experience, professional experience, internal materials (company files) and interviews, external materials (published literature) and interviews, and field research (observation, experiments, and surveys).

Wherever you need to go for your particular project, certain fact-finding guidelines are helpful. (The introduction, "Essentials of Successful Writing," describes many useful sources and procedures.) Sources of information are more plentiful than most people realize: your own organization, other business organizations, trade and professional associations, schools and research facilities, clubs and social-business organizations, government offices, specialized and general libraries, and selected segments of the public.

Original research can be tailored exactly to your needs. You can set up your own experiments, conduct your own surveys, make your own observations, and analyze the results. To help you collect data, you can design your own forms for you or your subjects to complete and use whatever forms and other materials you want to prepare.

Computerized search services such as NTIS (National Technical Information Service), ASI (American Statistics Index), and ABI/INFORM (Abstracted Business Information) save time when you need to

(LETTERHEAD)

FOR IMMEDIATE RELEASE

Chicago, Ill. (Sept. 4). _____

_____

_____

_____

_____

_____

_____

_____

_____

_____

_____

_____

-30-

News Release Format

check a huge number of data bases and abstracts. The computer does the tedious task of locating sources of information in relevant subject areas. When a library offers computerized search services, you simply tell the librarian key words that describe topics of interest to you, and the computer will provide a list of citations or abstracts, depending upon which data base you search through. Costs for using the service depend on the amount of time you use and the number of citations you need. Ask the librarian to explain the charges for your particular project.

Some fact finding you can conduct from your own office merely by using the Yellow Pages and your telephone. For interviews, you will likely visit someone else's office. If the subject doesn't object, you may want to use a tape recorder and camera. Forms (which you design yourself) are helpful for recording information you need and for helping you remember what questions to ask and in which sequence to ask them. But it is a mistake to adhere to a rigid outline of questions so strictly that you miss opportunities to pursue spontaneous avenues of thought. Leave space on your form or have plenty of paper available to explore unexpected revelations.

Library research is confusing to many people, primarily because they are not familiar with the procedures for locating necessary source material. Business research usually begins in the reference room, where standard reference works are arranged by subject on tables and shelves. The card catalog and periodical card files list all books and bound volumes of periodicals in the library by author, title, and subject. Professional writers often record the full facts of publication for each source they consult on a separate 3- by 5-inch card. Later these cards can be alphabetized by author or title for quick and easy reference in typing bibliographies and footnotes. Professional writers like to keep notes they take on each subject separate, again to make it easy for alphabetic or other form of organization later, when it is time to write the rough draft.

Most serious research will require a lot of digging, often through little-known books, periodicals, pamphlets, and other material. But it will help you to feel at home if the reference section of the library if you become familiar with some well-known business publications, directories, and indexes. Use the latest edition of books listed below. Always use the latest edition of anything you consult.

Guides to Business Sources

Some books tell you where to find other sources of information:

Business Information Sources, by Lorna Daniels (University of California Press)

Encyclopedia of Business Information Sources, edited by Paul Wasserman (Gale Research Co.)

How to Use the Business Library, with Sources of Business Information, by H. W. Johnson and S. W. McFarland (South-Western Publishing Co.)

Directories

Names of executives, companies, products, sales volume, and various other data are found in directories such as these:

American Medical Directory (American Medical Association)

Directory of Corporations, Directors, and Executives (Standard and Poor's Corp., McGraw-Hill)

Gale's Encyclopedia of Associations (Gale Research Co.)

Hotel and Motel Red Book (American Hotel Association Directory Corp.)

Martindale-Hubbell Law Directory (Martindale-Hubbell)

Million Dollar Directory (Dun and Bradstreet)

N. W. Ayer & Son's Directory of Newspapers and Periodicals (N. W. Ayer & Son)

Official Airline Guide (R. H. Donnelley)

Official Congressional Directory (U.S. Government Printing Office)

Official Guide of the Railways (National Railway Publications Co.)

Patterson's American Education (Educational Directories)

Poor's Register of Corporations, Directors, and Executives of the United States and Canada (Standard and Poor's Corp.)

Thomas' Register of American Manufacturers (Thomas Publishing Co.)

Ulrich's International Periodicals Directory (R. R. Bowker Co.)

U.S. Government Organization Manual (U.S. Government Printing Office)

Indexes

Book, newspaper, and periodical indexes will lead you to published books and articles on every subject imaginable:

Applied Science and Technology Index (H. W. Wilson Co.)

Books in Print (R. R. Bowker Co.)

Business Periodicals Index (H. W. Wilson Co.)

New York Times Index (The New York Times Co.)

Public Affairs Information Service

Reader's Guide to Periodical Literature (H. W. Wilson Co.)

Wall Street Journal Index (Dow Jones and Co.)

Business and Financial Publications

In addition to specialized magazines and journals, these general business publications are often helpful to the business researcher:

Barron's; National Business and Financial Weekly (weekly)

Business Week (weekly)

Commercial and Financial Chronicle (semiweekly)

The Conference Board Business Record (monthly)

Consumer Reports (monthly)

Current Industrial Reports (quarterly or throughout the year)

Dun & Bradstreet Reference Book (bimonthly)

Dun's Review and Modern Industry (monthly)

Economic Indicators (monthly)

Federal Reserve Bulletin (monthly)

Fortune (monthly)

Harvard Business Review (monthly)

Monthly Labor Review (monthly)

Moody's Investor Service (e.g., *Bond Record, Manual of Investments, Industrial Manual, Handbook of Common Stocks*)

Nation's Business (monthly)

The New York Times (daily)

Prentice-Hall Federal Tax Guide (annual)

Standard and Poor's Corporation (e.g., *Standard Corporation Records, Standard and Poor's Trade and Securities Service,* and *Standard and Poor's Bond Guide*)

Survey of Current Business (monthly)

Value Line (loose-leaf service)

Wall Street Journal (daily)

Business Statistics

Yearbooks, almanacs, and other publications contain a variety of governmental and business statistical data:

Economic Almanac (National Industrial Conference Board)

Handbook of Basic Economic Statistics (Economic Statistics Bureau of Washington, D.C.)

Historical Statistics of the United States (U.S. Bureau of the Census)

Statistical Abstract of the United States (U.S. Bureau of the Census)

Statistical Yearbook (United Nations)

Reference librarians will direct you to sources specifically suitable for your research topic. Don't hesitate to ask for help.

Organizing the Topics

Learning how to make outlines will prevent a lot of headaches later in a writing project. Outlines are like road maps. They keep you on course and guide you toward the correct destination. Just imagine yourself in strange territory without a map. You could wander around endlessly before arriving at the proper place. The same thing may happen if you try to research and write without a predetermined plan. Although detailed, formal outlines are not right or necessary for every project or every writer, some sort of planning process will certainly help you chart your way through unfamiliar territory.

Information must be controlled and refined to be useful. A

mountain of unrelated facts and figures would be totally unmanageable. Only an amateur would blindly march over to the library to research a broad subject such as *insurance,* for example. The scope of such a subject must be narrowed to some manageable aspect. This type of limitation must be imposed before you start your research. Preparing an outline is a practical, visual means of confining a topic before you waste endless hours or days searching for information you can't realistically use anyway.

Few people can prepare a perfect outline before they do any research, but in most cases, anything is better than nothing. List the main topics you want to cover in your communication. Say that you need to prepare a report for your organization's board of directors on increasing employee commitment to organizational goals. It will simplify your research if you have in front of you a list of each major point (or topic) you want to discuss in the report. It will be even more helpful if you can organize these points in outline form making secondary points subordinate to primary topics:

   I. Introduction
       A. Recognizing commitment problems
       B. Using directive psychology to solve problems

  II. How to get employee commitment
       A. Stating goals clearly and precisely
       B. Soliciting employee opinions
       C. Soliciting employee assistance
       D. Asking for employee commitment

 III. Conclusions
       A. Enhancing employee pride
       B. Increasing quality production

The outline topics you use will likely become the subheads in your final report. Two levels of subheads are used in the above example, but you may need three or four levels. Or perhaps you will use only one level. The more complex you make your subject, the more you will need to subordinate the various topics, and the more you will rely on different levels of subheads to organize your report into logical, easy-to-follow sections.

Writers call a list of subheads and sub-subheads, such as the one shown above, a *topic outline.* Such outlines use brief descriptions, sometimes one or two words each, of topics you want to discuss. The topic outline you prepare before starting your research may need revision during and after you complete your research. But this need not concern you. Revision is the mark of a professional writer, something you want to do, not something you want to avoid doing.

If you begin your research with some sort of topic outline to guide you, your note taking can be organized to match your outline topics. This will be a big help later when you are ready to start writing the rough draft. Grouping your notes in categories matching those on your topic outline means everything will be already organized when you are ready to start writing. You can follow this plan whether you take your notes on index cards or sheets of paper.

Before you begin writing the first rough draft, refine your topic outline until you have every item in exactly the order you want it. Review the outline to see if any item should be rephrased, added, or deleted. The outline topics should be the basis for the subheads in your final report. If you revise your outline topics carefully, you may even be able to use them in your report word for word.

Prepare a parallel outline, one that expands each topic into a full sentence. This sentence should summarize or introduce what you plan to say under that heading in the actual report. All of these sentences can serve as the first sentence in each section of your report (although later you may rephrase some of them). For example, you might expand the topic outline shown above into the following sentence outline:

I.   Employees who are committed to their jobs do more work and better work in less time.
   A.   Management needs to recognize signs of weak job commitment that affect organizational goals.
   B.   By using directive psychology, management can increase job commitment.

II.   Finding ways to increase employee commitment is a top priority.
   A.   Stating goals clearly and precisely will eliminate problems that arise from misunderstandings.
   B.   Soliciting employee opinions will increase the employee's sense of self-esteem.
   C.   Soliciting employee assistance will further motivate the employee to become involved.
   D.   Asking for a verbal commitment will make the goal more personal to the employee.

III.   Lack of employee commitment can cause production problems and must be overcome.

   A. Enhancing the employee's pride will stimulate
       increased commitment to organizational goals.
   B. Greater job commitment will increase and improve
       production.

Now you are ready to spread your notes before you and start adding
more sentences under each topic sentence. You are ready to start writing your first rough draft.

Writing and Editing Your Copy

Writing is different from something such as posting entries in
books of account. Instead of following a fairly standard procedure,
writers usually develop work habits that best suit them personally.
Some people can only compose at a typewriter. Others have to write
everything in longhand until it is almost perfect and then type it. Some
people can organize everything in advance so well that their first draft
needs very little revision and correction. But most writers need to prepare and revise their copy at least two or three times before everything
is clear, accurate, and readable. Always follow the procedure that best
suits you, but pay special need to the old familiar saying: "Amateurs
write; professional *rewrite*."

If your writing work habits are not well established, try building
upon your sentence outline (see the section "Organizing the Topics,"
page 166). Say that you are writing a report and you want the main
body of the report to run about ten pages. If you have five subheads on
your topic outline and therefore five sentences on your sentence outline, each major section of your report should average about two
pages. (Some pages may be shorter or longer.) Estimate how many
sentences will make up a typed, double-spaced page on the typewriter
that will be used to prepare your final manuscript. Perhaps you will
have fifteen sentences on each page. Obviously you will aim for about
thirty sentences (average) in each section. So under that first sentence
taken from your sentence outline, you will be writing about thirty sentences divided into two, three, or more paragraphs. Or perhaps the
thirty sentences can be divided and grouped under new sub-subheadings. No two pieces will be the same; this procedure is merely intended
as a general guideline. For those who worry about the creative aspect
of writing, this procedure is one way to convert a writing project into a
practical, routine business task. For others who have trouble getting
started, this procedure is an easy way to get those first words on paper.

If writing is new to you or difficult, don't try to make those first sentences perfect. Simply get the facts you want to present listed under each major sentence taken from the sentence outline. Later, when you rework everything for your second draft, you can start correcting grammar and dividing the sentences into paragraphs. The so-called writer's block often comes from the misconception that a first draft should look and sound nearly perfect. Try thinking about the professional house painter who has a contract to paint white over dark brown. Can you imagine how horrible the first coat will look? But the painter knows (I hope) that the house will look much better with the second coat, and if a third coat is needed, it will probably look absolutely beautiful. The painter should not despair after applying the first coat of paint, and you should not despair after writing the first draft of your communication.

While you are getting all of your first sentences hastily written out under each major sentence taken from the outline, mark anything you are quoting as a reminder to add a footnote at the bottom of the page. Some writers prefer to put all footnotes in numerical order under the subheading "Notes" at the end of the report just before the bibliography. (Notice the examples of credit lines supplied by copyright holders in the section "Handling Tables and Charts," below.) Whether you put footnotes at the bottom of the pages of text or collect them in a separate section at the end just before the bibliography, be consistent in the style you use and give full data the first time a source is cited. After the first time, a short reference or the abbreviation ibid. may be used. For example:

1. Jeffrey Steele, Marketing Today (New York: The Business Press, 1980), pp. 221–22.

2. Ibid.

3. Martha Benson, "Recession Insights," Economic Trends Journal 2 (March 1981): 300–301.

4. Steele, Marketing Today, p. 6.

5. Dennis Harline Holmes, in "Art and Contemporary Thought," in Art History, ed. René Mojeau (San Francisco: New Art Publishing, 1979), pp. 398–401.

6. Sally Anne Carrasci, "Territory and Property Rights" (Ph.D. diss., New York University, 1972), pp. 16–23.

7. Holmes, "Art and Contemporary Thought," p. 402.

8. Abraham Felshire, "Industry's New Kingpins" (Paper

delivered at the Thirty-sixth Annual Meeting of the Industry Analysts Society, Detroit, Michigan, August 21, 1978), p. 14.

9. Ibid., p. 15.

If you are working in a particular field, use the style preferred in that field. The Council of Biology Editors, for instance, has a stylebook called the *CBE Style Manual* (published by the American Institute of Biological Sciences in Washington, D.C.). For all other purposes, one of the best stylebooks is A *Manual of Style* (The University of Chicago Press). Stylebooks offer guidelines in spelling, capitalization, punctuation, footnote and bibliographic references, indexing, and many other technical aspects of writing and editing.

Prepare your illustrations as described in the next section, "Handling Tables and Charts," first preparing in rough form anything you intend to put in your communication. Once it is all together, you are ready to start correcting and polishing.

Since typesetters, printers, and other professionals use standard proofreading marks on manuscripts, galley proofs, and page proofs, it is a good idea to become familiar with these symbols (see the list in the section "Arranging for Printing and Production," below) and use them to edit your rough drafts.

Before you worry about smaller details such as spelling and punctuation, check some of the larger matters such as paragraphing. Have you broken the text of your rough draft into logical paragraphs? Does each paragraph begin with a topic sentence that summarizes a main point and introduces the discussion in that paragraph? Are the sentences arranged logically in the paragraph to lead readers to the concluding sentence? Does one paragraph slide nicely into the next or does a more logical link need to be established? Are the transitions smooth?

After you have your sentences in order, your paragraphs organized, and all desired facts and figures included, you can turn to the other miscellaneous aspect of editing. Many writers like to have something in front of them to remind them about the many details that need correcting. A standard checklist—something you can photocopy and keep in your desk drawer—might help. Such a list might use a key word or two for each step in the editing process. The word *paragraphs* might be meant to remind you to check whether you have logical breaks, a good lead sentence for each paragraph, a good concluding sentence for each paragraph, logical succession of sentences within the paragraph, and smooth transitions from one paragraph to another. Since writing projects differ radically, and since the skills of writers vary widely, one person's checklist might be different from or longer than someone else's checklist. Some or all of the following items might be on the checklist of most writers. (*Front matter* refers to the title page and table of contents; *end matter* refers to the appendix and bibliography.)

( ) Front matter	( ) Voice (active or passive)
( ) Opening (narrative hook)	( ) Conciseness
( ) Sections, subdivisons	( ) Clichés
( ) Paragraphs	( ) Irrelevancies
( ) Sentences	( ) Clarity
( ) Ending	( ) Preciseness
( ) Footnotes	( ) Pomposity
( ) End matter	( ) Vogue words
( ) Format	( ) Jargon
( ) Illustrations	( ) Gobbledygook
( ) Grammar	( ) Euphemisms
( ) Spelling	( ) Prefixes, suffixes
( ) Punctuation	( ) Trite expressions
( ) Capitalization	( ) Discrimination
( ) Word Choice	

After you are satisfied that you have thoroughly checked your draft for problems in one of the areas listed on your checklist, simply check off that item and move on to the next one (if you make photocopies of a standard list, you can use one for each project and discard it when you are finished).

Put as many things on your checklist as you can think of that trouble you or may weaken your message if you aren't reminded to be on guard for them. Other chapters in this book tell you what to look for in relation to each item on the list: chapter 1 tells you how to handle problems such as using prefixes and suffixes unnecessarily; chapter 2 consists of a list of words that are often used incorrectly in business writing; chapter 3 covers problems in spelling, punctuation, and capitalization; and chapter 4 explains how writing unintentionally can be discriminatory.

Reread your draft(s) and look for problems in all of the areas on your checklist, but not all at once. You will overlook something if you try to cope with more than one or a few things at a time. It is hard, for example, to be studying the content for clarity and watching for inconsistencies in capitalization at the same time. That word *inconsistencies* is important too. Readers will be puzzled and annoyed if you capitalize something such as *Socialist* in one sentence and later begin it with a small letter.

Mark your drafts heavily. Be as ruthless as you can with your editing. Don't worry if your sentences look like this; you want to improve everything possible:

The three important arrangements to make
~~There are four ways to proceed and handle this matter~~
are reviewing   preparing   and
~~such as, picking~~ a meeting room, ~~making~~ the room ~~ready,~~

organizing the meeting material, etc.

Some writers mark up their drafts so heavily that they always triple-space each draft to allow more room for rephrasing, rearranging, and correcting the sentences. This is fine. Do what is best for you. Above all, keep polishing. Do not think that the need for heavy rewriting or editing means you cannot write well. Keep telling yourself, "Amateurs write; professionals *rewrite*." (More information on marking manuscripts and typeset material is given in the section "Arranging for Printing and Production," page 177.) Although time is always a problem in a busy business office, try to organize your schedule so you can put your final draft aside overnight or for a couple days before it is typed. You may be able to read it more objectively later, and errors that you missed earlier may suddenly be obvious.

Handling Tables and Charts

Tables, charts, graphs, maps, and other illustrations often help readers comprehend information more easily. Some writers add illustrations to their reports and articles that are purely cosmetic. Such material contributes nothing useful or essential to the text of the communication. Instead, it weakens the presentation and should be deleted. But tables and charts that condense material, dramatize material, and supplement textual discussions with pertinent data are often desirable.

Charts, graphs, and other illustrations usually are identified by a *caption* or *legend*. Captions are titles set above or below the illustration, and legends are explanations, usually set below the illustration. Some figures combine both captions and legends below the illustrations:

> Figure 1. Relationship of demand for fuel to supply expectation. In each example shown here, demand increases as supply is expected to decrease.

> Figure 2. New developments in water safety. The instructor in this photograph is demonstrating new water-safety techniques developed by the Winslow Institute.

When an illustration already contains adequate explanatory information, only the word *Figure* and the appropriate number are needed: Figure 7.

Some large reports have several chapters, and figures may be labeled according to the chapter number. Figure 2–1 would thus be the first illustration in the second chapter and Figure 4–6 would be the sixth illustration in the fourth chapter.

Reports with a lot of illustrations should have a separate section called "List of Illustrations." It should follow the table of contents and should be typed in the same format, with the illustration number, title, and page number:

> Figure 1–1.   Machine Output by Region 3

You might combine tables and figures in one list or, if you have enough of each, prepare two separate lists.

Illustrations reprinted from or drawing upon information in the original source should have credit lines indicating the source of the material. If your report or article will be published, remember to write to the copyright holder for permission to reproduce outside material. (This procedure is essential for quoted material in the text as well.) Credit lines for copyrighted material may go at the end of the legend in parentheses or beneath the bottom edge of the illustration. Some copyright holders require that you use a specific form in your credit line. Otherwise, credit lines should be consistent in style on all illustrations. The following are examples of credit lines involving copyrighted material:

> Courtesy of The Landis Gallery.

> Adapted from T. M. Hill, <u>Nuclear Power</u> (Memphis: N. Wagner Publications, 1980), table 13.

Source: From Kay and Scott Balinger, <u>Skulduggery</u>, p. 60. Reprinted by permission of the authors. © 1977 by The Circle Press, Atlanta, Georgia.

Always make reference in the text discussion to any illustrations you include so readers are encouraged to look at each illustration at the most appropriate time. Mentioning such material in the text discussion also helps typesetters and printers know where to position the illustrations when they prepare your copy for publication. Some writers like to have their tables and charts positioned throughout the text; others prefer to collect all illustrations at the end of a report so the reader can follow the text more easily without visual distraction. Use your own judgment and aim to make things easiest for the reader (not for you).

Like charts and graphs, tables also vary widely. Frequently they have a table number and title, a top row (or rows) of column heads, and a left-hand list of items called the *stub*. Immediately beneath the table is the source note followed by table footnotes, if any (see the example on page 176).

If you have several tables in your material, check each one for consistency in layout and stylistic matters. Does each major word in all column heads begin with a capital letter? Does the first word in each item of the stub begin with a capital letter? Whatever style you adopt, stick with it. Rule your tables consistently too. For the sake of simplicity and lower costs in typesetting material, many writers use only horizontal rules—a single or double rule after the table title, a single rule after the column heads, and a single or double rule after the table body. (See the example on page 176.) Source notes and footnotes are placed below the table after the final rule.

In statistical matter, always align dollar signs, percent signs, decimals, and other symbols:

```
$   6,211.70
  135,090.62
      275.04
   14,983.99
```

You need to give the dollar sign or percent sign only once at the top of the column:

```
13%
 9
27
15
 3
```

Table 2-3

Comparison of Office Reproduction Processes
by Quantity and Quality of Copies

Process	Recommended Quantity per Run	Quality Range of Copies
Fluid duplicator	to 500	fair
Stencil duplicator	to 3,000	fair to good
Offset duplicator	to 10,000	good to excellent
Photocopier	to 100[a]	fair to excellent[b]

Source: Office Equipment Supply Depot.

Note: Both quantity and quality vary greatly according to manufacturer, individual machine, and user skill.

[a] Other methods of reproduction may be more suitable if runs continually reach 100 copies.

[b] Also facsimile and art reproduction in advanced models.

Table Format

In long columns of statistics with zero preceding the decimal, you may omit all zeros except one at the top and one at the bottom of the column (if possible, carry all decimal fractions to the same number of places):

```
0.022
 .105
 .226
 .300
 .792
 .458
 .700
0.311
```

Some writers call everything a table or a figure. But you should distinguish between purely tabular matter and other graphic illustrations. If any illustration appears too complex, break it up into several figures or tables. The same rule that applies to your general writing applies to the preparation of tables and charts: Keep them short and simple.

Arranging for Printing and Production

Some reports must be typeset and printed, so you need to become familiar with the basic steps in arranging for the production of your manuscript.

Marking Copy

To prepare your manuscript for production, you need to type it double-spaced, mark final editorial corrections, and mark various typesetting instructions. Use the proofreader chart shown in this section and mark your copy as shown below:

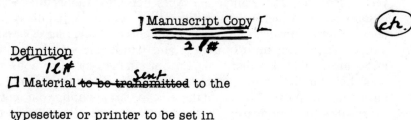

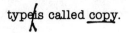

Write and circle instructions to the typesetter or printer in the margins. Make type corrections directly on the manuscript in and above the lines of type. Cross out words to be deleted and write the new words directly above. Separate two words run together with a vertical line between them. To retain material, add a row of dots beneath the crossed-out words and circle the word *stet* in the margin.

To determine type size and style, ask the typesetter to give you a book of samples. Don't hesitate to ask for recommendations and advice on marking the specifications. Typefaces have names such as Times Roman and Bodoni. They come in a variety of sizes described by *points*. One inch equals six picas, and a point is one-twelfth of a pica. So you can see that a point is not very large. The space between lines (leading) is also measured in points. But column widths are indicated by picas. Consider the instructions to the typesetter in the above example to set the paragraph text (except for the subheads) in 10/12 Times Roman X36: the number 10 means you want a 10-point type size; 12 means you want 2 points leading between lines; 36 means you want the text column to be 36 picas wide.

Typesetters use ems and ens too. An *em* is the square of the height of the body of any type size. This is a one-em dash (—). An *en* is one-half of an em. This is a one-en dash (–). Mark such dashes with the symbol $\frac{1}{M}$ or $\frac{1}{N}$. Also mark other things such as spacing around subheads and paragraph indentation. Paragraphs, for instance, might be indented two picas or one em, whatever looks attractive for your size page and the type style. The above example shows that the headline is to be centered in all capital letters, with two line spaces beneath the major head and one line space beneath the secondary head. The paragraph in the example is marked for a one-pica indentation.

Processing Proofs

After the typesetter has set your copy, you will receive either galley proofs or page proofs. *Galley proofs* are proofs of typeset copy not yet divided into pages. Printers and typesetters often supply three sets to customers, one which you must correct and return. When the typeset copy is already divided into pages, the proofs are called *pages* or *page proofs*. Again, you need to correct and return one set. Typesetting errors are corrected without charge, but changes or corrections you make here for the first time involve new work for the typesetter and are an additional charge. This is not the time to start rewriting your report. Make your corrections using the proofreader marks illustrated in the section "Marking Copy." Typeset galleys and pages usually do not have room between lines to make editorial corrections, so you need to mark them in the margins like this:

Proofreader Marks

In Margin	In Text	Meaning
ℒ	columns	Delete
ℰ	columns	Delete and close up
stet.	writing reports	Let it stand
no ¶	chapters. Examples show	No paragraph
#	spellingand	Add space
out, sc	actual ᴧ of the	Something missing; see copy
sp. out	4 people	Spell out
⌒	infor mation	Close up
[	[discuss it	Move left
]	discuss it	Move right
tr.	indcative	Transpose
‖	arrange the tables and	Line up
¶	editing. However	New paragraph
?	1984	Question to author
?	what to do	Insert question mark
!	Great	Insert exclamation mark
⸗	non European	Insert hyphen
❞/❞	as she said, Now.	Insert quotation marks
;	revision therefore	semicolon

Proofreader Marks (Continued)

In Margin	In Text	Meaning
	the following items	Insert colon
	one, two and three	Insert comma
	this material	Insert period
	the readers viewpoint	Insert apostrophe
	ˈook	Change to b
Caps (or ≡)	Introduction	Set in capital letters
lc	PREFACE	Set in lowercase letters
bf (or ‿)	Writing and Editing	Set in boldface type
ital. (or —)	Copyediting Handbook	Set in italic type
s.c. (or =)	B.C. or A.D.	Set in small capitals
c. or s.c.	Writing Manual	Set in caps and small caps
⌄⌄	k e y topics	Correct uneven spacing
⑨	ɹey topics	Upside down
□	□Describe the process	Indent one em
rom.	headings	Change to roman type
³	footnote 3	Set as superior number
₁	c 5	Set as inferior number
[/]	a + b	Insert brackets
(/)	a + b	Insert parentheses
¹⁄M	and chapters--these	one-em dash

Typesetters and printers can help you select sizes and
styles of type some of them provide free type books.[2]

Be certain to check other matters too such as paragraph indentation, space around subheads, and pagination. Read all figure legends, check the position of tables, and see whether facing pages are of equal length. Very short lines called *widows* should not be carried to the top of a new page, and footnotes must be placed at the bottom of the appropriate pages (unless they are collected in a "Notes" section at the end of the report). Look at everything. Is the typeface the correct size and style? Are unacceptable rivers of white space flowing across and up and down the pages? Are lines blurred? Did the typesetter accidentally slip in a different typeface for one letter or word?

After you are certain everything is marked for correction, return your marked proofs and wait for the next stage, probably a negative proof (often called a *blueprint* or *whiteprint*) showing everything as it is ready for printing. Examine this proof carefully too. The typesetter may have overlooked some corrections you marked on the galleys or pages. Or the printer may have the negative proof pages out of order. Be as critical as possible throughout each stage, because once the material is printed, it is too late to start all over (unless you have lots of time and money).

Working with Outsiders

Writing and editing a report is one thing, but preparing illustrations and typesetting and printing the report are something else. At some point, you will need to rely on others, and it helps to know exactly what you want, how much you (or your organization) can afford to spend, and where to go for the help you need.

Perhaps your organization has an art department, a photographer and a darkroom, and even typesetting and printing equipment. But you still must be able to instruct the people who will do the work. Most likely you will have to check the Yellow Pages and call a free-lance artist and a photographer and use an outside typesetter and printer. No matter where you look, in-house or outside, don't hesitate to ask for advice. The people you consult are professionals in their respective fields. You may want a four-color photograph, for example, but a competent photographer should be able to suggest other satisfactory but less costly alternatives.

Whatever you do, get quotes. If possible, get several quotes, because free-lancers and printers do not always charge standard rates. They do not always do standard quality work either, so ask to see samples and find out whether they will guarantee delivery on schedule. On the other hand, it is also important to respect their needs and limitations. If you pressure an artist to prepare illustrations at breakneck speed, the result may look like something thrown together in the dark. Use your best judgment. But temper your expectations with reason and enhance your ability to work successfully with outsiders by increasing your knowledge of printing and production.

Most of the rules and guidelines that apply to report and article writing apply to all types of writing. One thing is certain: anything that will put you on the road to better business writing will also put you on the road to a more successful business career.

INDEX

A *while* 44
Abbreviations
  Acronyms 101
  Agencies and Organizations 98–99
  to Avoid 98
  in Body of Message 98
  in Business Writing 97–103
  Consistency 97
  Countries 102
  Esq. 101
  in Footnotes and Bibliographies 101–2
  Popular Expressions 101
  Prominent Persons 101
  in Specialized Writing 102–3
  States 100
  Titles 101
  United States 102
  Use of Period 84–85
ABI/INFORM 161
Ability 44
About 45
Abridged 45
Abstract
  in Reports 154
Abstract Words 25

Abstracted Business Information 161
Accept 45
Accidentally 45
Accidently 45
Acknowledge 45
Acknowledgment Letter 143
Acronyms 101
Action Verbs
  See Active Voice
Active Voice
  in Conversation 11
  for Direct, Concise, Personal Messages 14
  Pattern for 10
  Shifting of Voice 13–14
  to Warn or Instruct 11
Acts
  Capitalization of 89
Adapt 45
Address
  Addressing Women 122–24
  Inside Address 140
  Name and Gender Unknown 123
  Organizations of Men and Women 123
  in Word Division 77

Adept 45
Adjectives
   Hyphenation 82
   in Publicity Releases 161
Adjustment Letters 145
Admit 45
Adopt 45
Adverb
   Hyphenation 82
Adverse 46
Advertising
   Openings 22
   Precise Language 26–27
   Use of Active Sentences 14
   Use of Exclamation Point 82
Advice 46
Advise 46
Affect 46
Affectation
   See Pompous Writing
Affirmative Action Requirements
   118
Afflict 46
Agencies
   Abbreviation of 99
Aid 46
Aim 47
All ready 47
All right 47
All together 47
Already 47
Alright 47
Alter 47
Although 47
Altogether 47
Amend 48
Amendments
   Capitalization of 89
American Medical Directory 164
American Statistics Index 161
Among 48
Anecdotes 21–22
Anxious 48
Anybody 48

Anyone 48
Apology Letter 145
Apostrophe
   with Names 78–79
   to Show Omission 79
   to Show Possession 78–79
Appearance
   of Letters and Memos 131,
      133
   Spelling, Punctuation, and
      Capitalization 73, 86
Appendix 153, 154, 158
*Applied Science and Technology
   Index* 165
Appointment Letter 143
Appraise 48
Appreciation Letters 144–45
Apprise 48
Apt 48
Around 45
Articles
   Benefits 157
   Magazine Requirements 157
   Queries 157
   Submission 157
   Typing 157–58
As 49
As . . . as 49
As if 49
As though 49
ASI 161
Assist 46
Assure 49
Attention Line
   in Letters 133
Attitude
   in Letters and Memos 129–
      31
   in Nondiscriminatory Writing
      114–27
Audience
   See Reader
Averse 46
Avoiding Stereotypes 115

Awards
  Capitalization of 92–93
Awhile 44

Balance 49
Barely 50
*Barrons, National Business and
    Financial Weekly* 165
Because 50
Begin 50
Beginnings
  Anecdotes 21–22
  First Impression 21
  Formal Introductions 22
  Good Taste 22
  Insights into Message 23
  Letters and Memos 131–32
  Narrative Hook 21
  Objectives 21
  Questions 23
  as a Response 22
  Teasers 22
  Use of Statistics 22
Beside 50
Besides 50
Between 48
Bible
  Capitalization of 95
Bibliographies 6
  in Reports 154
  in Research 163
  Use of Abbreviations in 97
Bilateral 51
Bills
  Capitalization of 89
Block Format
  in Letters 135
Blueprint 181
Body
  of Letters 139
  of Report 154
Boldface
  Proofreader Marks 180

Books in Print 165
Brackets
  with Parentheses 79
Brochure 51
Business Communication
  See Writing
Business Information Sources 164
Business Periodicals Index 165
Business Publications 165
Business Week 165
Business Writing
  See Writing

Can 51
Candid 51
Canvas 51
Canvass 51
Capacity 44
Capital 51
Capital Letters
  Proofreader Marks 180
Capitalization
  Abbreviations 97–103
  Appearance 86–87
  Consistency 87
  Education 87–88
  Geography 88–89
  Government and Politics 89
  History 90–91
  Holidays, Festivals, and Seasons
    91
  Judiciary 91–92
  Listings and Outlines 92
  Military 92–93
  Numbers 93
  Proper Nouns 93–94
  Religion 95
  Titles of Persons 95–96
  Titles of Works 96–97
  Trends in 86
Capitol 51
Caps and Small Caps
  Proofreader Marks 180

Captions 174
Carbon-Copy Notation
  with Letters and Memos 139
Card Catalog 163
CBE Style Manual 171
Censor 52
Censure 52
Change 47
Charts
  See Tables
Checklist
  in Drafting 171–72
Churches
  Capitalization of 95
Civil Rights Act of 1964 121, 127
Clarity
  Factors Affecting 18–20
  Letters and Memos 128
  Punctuation 77–86
  for Reader 18–19, 173
  References to Handicapped
      Persons 120
  Use of Subheads 153
Classes, School
  Capitalization of 87
Clichés 15–16
  Ethnic Clichés 110
Client 52
Close 52
Close Up
  Proofreader Marks 179
Closing
  See Ending
Collection Letters 145–46
Colleges
  Capitalization of 87
Colon
  to Introduce a List 80
  after Salutations 79
  to Separate Data 79
  to Show Pause 80
  to Show Ratios and Time 80
Comma
  for Clarity 81

  with Nonrestrictive Clauses 80
  to Separate Words 80
  to Set off Appositives 80
  to Set off Introductory Words 81
  to Set off Quotations 80
  to Show Omission 80
Commence 50
*Commercial and Financial
    Chronicle* 165
Common 52
Communication
  See Writing
Comparatively 53
Compare 53
Complaint Letters 145
Complement 53
Complementary 53
Compliment 53
Complimentary Close
  in Letters 139
Compose 53
Compound Words
  Hyphenation 82–83
  Plurals 105
Comprise 53
Concept 54
Conciseness 15–18
  in Letters and Memos 131
Conclusion
  See Endings
*Conference Board Business Record,
    The* 165
Confidential Notation
  in Letters 140
Conjunctions
  Punctuation 77
Connotation 24, 54
Consistency
  Abbreviations 97
  in Spelling, Punctuation, and
    Capitalization 73, 87, 97
  in Style 18
  in Word Usage 44
Consistently 54

Consonants
in Spelling 104–9
Constantly 54
Constitutions
Capitalization of 89
Consumer Reports 165
Continual 54
Continuation Pages
for Letters and Memos 139
Continue 54
Continuous 54
Contractions
Use of Apostrophe 79
in Word Division 76
Contrast 53
Conversational Words
in Reference to Handicapped 119
Tone in Letters and Memos
130–31
Copyrighted Material 174–75
Corrections
Marking 177–81
Correspondence
See Letters, Memos
Costs
See Quotations
Countries
Abbreviation of 102
Capitalization of 88
Courses, School
Capitalization of 87
Courts
Capitalization of 91–92
Cover Page
for Proposals 158
Cover Sheet
for Proposals 158
Covert 55
Convince 55
Craft, Military
Capitalization of 92–93
Credible 55
Credit Letters 145–46
Credit Lines 174–75

Creditable 55
Cultural Periods
Capitalization of 90–91
Curiosity 21
Current Industrial Reports 165
Currently 55
Customary 55
Customer 52

Dash
for Emphasis 81
to Show Interruption 81
in Word Division 77
Data-Recording Procedures 4, 163
Dateline
in Letters 139
in Publicity Releases 160
Dates
Punctuation in Citations 79, 154
Decisive 55
Deduction 55
Defer 56
Degree 56
Degrees, Academic
Abbreviations 101
Capitalization of 87
Deity
Capitalization of 95
Delay 56
Deletion
Proofreader Marks 179
Denotation 24, 54
Deny 56
Departments
Capitalization of 87
Depositary 56
Depository 56
Dictionary
Abbreviations 103
Spelling 113
Word Division 74
Word Use 44, 104
Different from 56

Different than 56
Different to 56
Differentiate 57
Directories 164
Directory of Corporations, Directors,
    and Executives 164
Disability 57
Discrimination
    See Nondiscriminatory
        Communication
Disinterested 57
Disorganized 57
Displace 57
Disqualified 58
Disregardless 58
Dissatisfied 58
Distinguish 57
Documents
    Capitalization of 90–91
Doubt if 58
Doubt that 58
Doubt whether 58
Drafts
    Checklist 171–72
    Illustrations 171, 173–77
    Outlines 5–6, 166–70
    Preparing 5–8
    Writing and Editing 169–77
Due to 50
Dun & Bradstreet Reference Book
    165
Dun's Review and Modern Industry
    165

Each other 58
Eager 48
Economic Almanac 166
Economic Indicators 165
Editing
    See Revision
Education
    Capitalization in 87
Effect 46

Effective 58
Effectual 58
Efficient 58
Elicit 59
Ellipses
    to Show Omission 82
    Spacing Around 82
Em Dash 178
Emend 48
Emigrate 59
Eminent 59
En Dash 178
Enclosure Notation
    in Letters and Memos 140
Encyclopedia of Business
        Information Sources 164
End Matter 172
    in Reports 153
Endings
    Length 23
    Letters and Memos 132–33
    Objectives 23
    Providing Answers 24
Endless 59
Ensure 49
Envelopes
    Address 140
    Mail Notation 140
    Personal or Confidential Notation
        140
Envisage 59
Envision 59
Epithets
    Capitalization of 93–94
Equal Employment Opportunity
        Commission 118
Equal Pay Act of 1963 121
Especial 60
Esquire
    Abbreviation of 101
Essential 60
Essentially 60
Euphemism 33
Everybody 60

Everyone 60
Example 60
Except 45
Exclamation Point
    for Irony 82
    to Show Strong Feeling 82
Explicit 61
Extended 61
Extensive 61
Extent 56
Extract 85

Farther 61
Fashion 61
Feasible 61
Federal Reserve Bulletin 165
Festivals
    Capitalization of 91
Fewer 62
Figures
    See Statistics
Financial Publications 165
First 62
Firstly 62
Follow-up Letters 146
Footnotes
    Drafting 170, 174–75
    in Research 163
    Short References 170
    Use of Abbreviations in 97
Foreword
    in Reports 154
Format
    Articles 157
    Letters and Memos 133–38
    Proposals 158
    Releases 158, 160, 162
    Reports 153–57
Forms
    in Research 4, 163
Fortune 165
Frank 51
Freelancers 177–82

Frequent 62
Front Matter 172
Full-Block Format
    in Letters 134
Further 61

Gale's Encyclopedia of Associations
    164
Galley Proof 178
Geography
    Capitalization in 88–89
Geological Periods
    Capitalization of 90–91
Gloomy 62
Gobbledygook 33
Good 62
Goodwill Letters 144–45
Government
    Capitalization in 89–90
Grammar 62
Guarantee 63
Guaranty 63
*Guidelines for Creating Positive
    Sexual and Racial Images in
    Educational Materials* 115
*Guidelines for Equal Treatment of
    the Sexes in McGraw-Hill Book
    Company Publications* 126
*Guidelines for Newswriting About
    Women* 126
*Guidelines for Nonsexist Use of
    Language in NCTE
    Publications* 126

*Handbook of Basic Economic
    Statistics* 166
Handicapped Persons
    Attitudes Toward 118
    Claims of Discrimination 121
    Controversial Language 119
    Demeaning Connotations 119
    Educating the Public 121

Handicapped Persons (*Cont.*):
  Labels 119
  References to the Handicapped
    120–21
  Rehabilitation Act of 1973 121
  Stereotyping 120
  Vietnam Veterans Readjustment
    Act of 1974 121
Handle 63
Happen 63
Hardly 50
Harvard Business Review 165
Help 46
Historical Statistics of the United
  States 166
History
  Capitalization in 90–91
Holidays
  Capitalization of 91
Honors
  Capitalization of 87
Hotel and Motel Red Book 164
How to Use the Business Library,
  with Sources of Business
  Information 164
Hyphen
  in Adjectives 82–83
  in Adverbs 82–83
  in Numbers 82–83
  to Separate Compound Words
    82–84
  with Suffixes and Prefixes 83–84
  in Word Division 73–74

Idea 54
If 63
Illicit 59
Illustrations
  See Tables and Charts
Imagine 63
Immigrate 59
Imminent 59

Implicit 61
Imply 64
Impracticable 64
Impractical 64
Inability 57
Incidentally 64
Incidently 64
Incisive 55
Inconsistencies
  Checking for 173
Index Cards
  in Research 4, 154, 163
Indexes 165
Induction 55
Ineffective 64
Ineffectual 64
Infer 64
Inferior Number
  Proofreader Marks 180
Inflict 46
Ingenious 64
Ingenuous 64
Innumerable 59
Inquiry Letters 148
Inside Address
  in Letters 140
Instance 60
Insure 49
Intend 47
Interoffice Communication
  See Memo
Interviews 4
Introduction Letters 147
Introductions
  See Beginnings
Invitations 150–51
Irony 64
Irregardless 58
Irreversible 65
Irrevocable 65
Italics
  in Typeset Material 85
  Proofreader Marks 180

Jargon 33
Judicial 65
Judiciary
    Capitalization of 91–92
Judicious 65

Know 65

Labels 26
    Nondiscriminatory Writing 114–
        27
Lack 65
Language
    See Capitalization,
        Nondiscriminatory
        Communication,
        Punctuation, Spelling, Style,
        Words
    Also see specific word definitions
        (chapter 2)
Lawful 66
Laws
    Capitalization of 89
Leaflet 51
Legal 66
Legal Cases
    Capitalization of 91–92
Legends 174
Legislative Bodies
    Capitalization of 89
Less 62
Letter of Transmittal
    in Reports 154
Letters
    Acknowledgments 143
    Appearance 131
    Appointments 144
    Appreciation and Goodwill 144–
        45
    Attention Line 133
    Body 139

Carbon-Copy Notation 139
Complaints and Adjustments 145
Complimentary Close 139
Continuation Pages 139
Conversational Tone 130–31
Credit and Collection 145–46
Dateline 139
Enclosure Notation 140
Follow-up and Reminders 146–
    47
Format 133–38
Inside Address 140
Introductions and References
    147
Mail Notation 140
Objectives 128, 133
Personal or Confidential Notation
    140
Personal References 130–31
Positive Approach 130
Postscript 140
Reference Initials 141
Reference Line 141
Requests and Inquiries 148
Reservations and Orders 148–
    49
Sales Letters 149–50
Salutation 141
Signature 141–42
Social-Business Letters and
    Invitations 150–51
Stationery 133
Style and Tone 129–33
Subject Line 142
as Tools 128
You Attitude 129–31
Liable 48
Libel 66
Library Research 4, 163
Licit 59
Like 49
Likely 48
List of Illustrations 174

Lists
  Capitalization in 92
  of Illustrations 174
Locality 66
Location 66
Lowercase 86
Lowercase Letters
  Proofreader Marks 180
Luxuriant 66
Luxurious 66

Mail Notation
  in Letters 140
Maintain 66
Majority 66
Manage 63
Manner 61
Manual of Style, A 177
Manuscript
  See Articles, Proposals, Publicity
      Releases, Reports
Martindale-Hubbell Law Directory
    164
May 51
Mechanics
  of Business Letters 133–42
Memo Format 138
  for Reports 153–54
  for Proposals 158–60
Memos
  Appearance 131
  Appointments 144
  Carbon-Copy Notation 139
  Continuation Pages 139
  Conversational Tone 130–31
  Dateline 139
  Enclosure Notation 140
  Follow-up 146–47
  Format 133, 138
  Guide Words 142
  Heading 142
  Objectives 128, 133

  Orders and Reservations 148–49
  Personal References 130–31
  Positive Approach 130
  Postscript 140
  Proposals 158–60
  Reference Initials 141
  Reports 153–54
  Style and Tone 129–33
  as Tools 128
  You Attitude 129–31
Messages
  See Writing
Meticulous 67
Military
  Capitalization in 92–93
Military Titles
  Capitalization of 92
Million Dollar Directory 164
Mimeographing
  Publicity Releases 161
Minority 66
Misplace 57
Miss
  in Addressing Women 122–23
  in Signatures 141
Mode 61
Model Letters and Memos 142–
    51
Modified-Block Format
  in Letters 136
Monthly Labor Review 165
Moody's Investor Service 165
Mrs.
  in Addressing Women 122–23
  in Signatures 141
Ms.
  in Addressing Women 122–23
  Magazine 127
Multi-Ethnic Guidelines 115
Mutual 52
Mysterious 67
Mystical 67
Mythical 67

National NOW Times 127
National Technical Information
 Service 161
Nation's Business 165
Near 52
Necessary 60
Need 65
Negative Proof 181
New York Times, The 166
New York Times Index 165
News Release
 See Publicity Releases
Nondiscriminatory Communication
 Addressing Women 122–25
 Affirmative Action Requirements
  118
 Books 115, 126
 Business Correspondence 122–23
 Civil Rights Act of 1964 121,
  127
 Equal Employment Opportunity
  Commission 118
 Equal Pay Act of 1963 121
 Equality toward Sexes 124, 127
 Ethnic Clichés 118
 Myths 116–17
 Name and Gender Unknown 123
 Negative Attitudes 115–16
 Negative Implications 116
 Patronizing 117
 Power of Suggestion 117
 Racial and Ethnic Bias 115–18
 Rehabilitation Act of 1973 121
 Respect for Handicapped 118–21
 Sensitivity 114–15
 Sexist References 125–26
 Sexual Bias 121–27
 Social Correspondence 122–23
 Stereotyping 115–16, 118, 120
 Tokenism 117–18
 Vietnam Veterans Readjustment
  Act of 1974 121
Nonrestrictive Clauses 80

Note Taking 163, 168
Notion 54
Nouns, Compound
 Plurals 105
NOW 127
NTIS 161
Numbers
 Capitalization of 93
 See also Statistics
N. W. Ayer & Son's Directory of
  Newspapers and Periodicals
  164

Occur 63
Official 67
Official Airline Guide 164
Official Congressional Directory 164
Official Guide of the Railways 164
Officious 67
Omission 68
One another 58
One's self 67
Oneself 67
Opening
 See Beginning
Oral 67
Order Letters 148
Organization
 of Topics 3, 5–6, 166–70
Outlines
 Capitalization in 92
 for Clarity 20
 Outline Expansion 6, 166–70
 Sentence Outline 5–6, 168–70
 Topic Outline 5, 166–69
Oversight 68
Overt 55

Pace 18, 20
Page Proof 178
Pamphlet 51

Paragraphs
  Final 132
Parentheses
  to Enclose Words and Figures 84
Part 68
Passive Voice
  to Avoid Embarrassment 12
  to Focus on Action 13
  for Indirect and Impersonal
    Messages 14
  Pattern for 10
  Shifting of Voice 13–14
  When Doer Is Unimportant 12
Patron 52
Patronizing
  Racial and Ethnic Discrimination
    115–18
Patterson's American Education 164
People 68
Period
  to End a Sentence 84–85
  in a List 84–85
  with Numbers and Abbreviations
    84–85, 97–103
Permissions
  See Copyrighted Material
Personal Notation
  in Letters 140
Personal References
  in Letters and Memos 130–31
Personnel Letter 147
Persons 68
Persuade 55
Pessimistic 62
Pica 178
Planning 2
Plurality 66
Plurals
  Nouns 104–5
  Words Ending in *ch, sh, ss, x*
    104
  Words Ending in *f, ff, fe* 104
  Words Ending in *o* 104–5
  Words Ending in *y* 104

Point 178
Point of view 68
Political Parties
  Capitalization of 89
Political Units
  Capitalization of 90
Politics
  Capitalization in 89–90
Pompous Writing 29–34
  List of Pompous Words 30
*Poor's Register of Corporations,
  Directors, and Executives of the
  United States and Canada* 164
Popular Names
  Capitalization of 88
Portion 68
Possible 61
Postal Abbreviations 100
Postpone 56
Postscript
  in Letters and Memos 140
Practicable 68
Practical 68
Precise Words
  in Sales Material 26
  Simple Language 28–29
  Use of 24–29
Prefixes 33–34
  with Proper Names 83–84
  Spelling 108–9
  in Word Division 75
Prejudice 26
  See also Nondiscriminatory
    Communication
Preliminary Pages
  in Reports 153
Prentice-Hall Federal Tax Guide
  166
Preparation
  for Writing 2
Prescribed 68
Presently 55
Press Release
  See Publicity Releases

Presumably 69
Principal 69
Principle 69
Printing 177–82
Procedures
  Research 3–4
  Writing 1–8
Production
  Marking Copy 177–78
  Processing Proofs 178–81
  Working with Outsiders 181–82
Pronounciation
  in Word Division 74
Proofreader Chart 179–80
Proofreading Marks 171, 173, 179–80
Proper Names
  Capitalization 93–94
  in Word Division 76
Proper Nouns
  Capitalization 93–94
Proposals
  Memo Format 158
  Solicited 158
  Subheads 158–60
  Unsolicited 158
Proscribed 68
Proved 69
Proven 69
Public Affairs Information Service 165
Publicity Releases
  Clichés 15
  Format 158, 160, 162
  Typing 161
Punctuation
  Apostrophe 78–79
  Brackets 79
  Colon 79–80
  Comma 80–81
  Dash 81
  Ellipses 82
  Exclamation Point 82
  Hyphen 82–84

Parentheses 84
Period 84–85
Question Marks 85
Quotation Marks 85–86
Semicolon 86
Trend in 77
Purposefully 69
Purposely 69

Qualitative 69
Quantitative 69
Queries
  for Articles 157
Question Marks
  to End a Direct Question 85
  to Show Doubt 85
Questionnaires
  in Interviews 4, 163
Questions
  as Introductions 23
  Question Mark 85
Quotation Marks
  to Enclose Precise Quotes 85–86
  with Extracts 85
  Single Quotation Marks 85
  with Slang 85–86
  in Typeset Material 85
Quotations
  in Printing 181

Races and Tribes
  Capitalization of 93–94
Racism 114–18
Racism in the English Language 115
Raise 69
Random House Guidelines for Multi-Ethnic/Nonsexist Survey 115
Reaction 70
Reader
  Closings 133

Reader (*Cont.*):
　Comprehension 9, 18–19, 173
　Helping 7, 8, 34, 131
　Openers 21
　Requirements of 8, 150
　You Attitude 129
Reader's Guide to Periodical
　　Literature 165
Realize 65
Rear 69
Recurring 62
Redundant 70
Reference Books
　Business and Financial
　　Publications 165–66
　Business Statistics 166
　Directories 164
　Guides to Business Sources
　Indexes 165
　Stylebooks 171
Reference Initials
　in Letters and Memos 141
Reference Letters 147
Reference Line
　in Letters 141
Reference Room
　Library 163
References
　See Bibliographies, Footnotes
Refute 56
Regions
　Capitalization of 88
Rehabilitation Act of 1973 121
Relatively 53
Religion
　Capitalization of 95
Remainder 49
Reminder Letters 146
Repair 66
Repetition 18
Reply 70
Reported 70
Reports
　Endings

Format and Style 153–57
Introductions 22
Long, Formal Reports 154
Memo Format 153–54
Paper 154
Short, Informal Reports 153–54
Typing 154, 157
Reputed 70
Requests 143, 146, 148
Research
　Bibliographies 6
　Business and Financial
　　Publications 165–66
　Business Statistics 166
　Computerized-Search Services
　　161–62
　Directories 164
　Footnotes 6
　Index Cards 4, 154, 163
　Indexes 165
　Interviews 163
　Library Research 163
　Original Research 161
　Outlines 5–6, 166–70
　Procedures of Information 4,
　　161, 163–64
　Subtopics 3, 166–70
　Topics 3, 166–70
Reservation Letters 148
Response 70
Resume 54
Revision 6–8
　Checklist for 7, 172
　Reader Requirements 8
　Reports 154
　Standards for 8, 173
Roman Type
　Proofreader Marks 180
Round 45

Sales Letters 149–50
Salutation
　in Letters 141

Sample 60
Sarcasm 64
Satire 64
Scarcely 50
Schools
  Capitalization of 87
Scope, of Information 2
Scrupulous 67
Seasons
  Capitalization of 91
Semiblock Format
  See Modified-Block Format
Semicolon
  with Commas 86
  to Separate Clauses 86
Sensitivity
  in Writing 114, 127
Sentences
  Active 10–15
  Clarity 18
  Outlines 5–6, 168–70
  Passive 10–15
  Punctuation 77–86
Service 66
Services, Religious
  Capitalization of 95
Sexual Bias
  Addressing Women 122–24
  Asexual Words 125
  Business Correspondence 122–23
  Civil Rights Act of 1964 121,
    127
  Equal Pay Act of 1963 121
  Name and Gender Unknown 123
  Organizations of Men and
    Women 123
  Sexist References 125
  Social Correspondence 122–23
  Trends 122
  Use of *Ms.* 122–23
Shall 70
Share 68
Short References
  in Footnotes 170–71

Shut 52
Signature
  in Letters 141–42
Simplified Format
  in Letters 137
Since 49
Slander 66
Slang 85
Small Capitals
  Proofreader Marks 180
So . . . as 49
Social-Business Letters 150–51
Source Notes 175
Sources of Information 4, 163–66
Special 60
Spelling
  Aids 104
  Errors 103
  Plurals 104–5
  Prefixes 108–9
  Suffixes and Other Word
    Endings 105–8
  Troublesome Words 109–13
Standard and Poor's Corporation
  166
Standpoint 68
States
  Abbreviations 100
Stationary 70
Stationery 70
  See also Letters
*Statistical Abstract of the United
  States* 166
Statistical Yearbook 166
Statistics
  Capitalization in 93
  Sources of 166
  Typing 175
  in Word Division 76
Stereotyping
  Persons with Handicaps 120
  Racial and Ethnic 115–18
Stet.
  Proofreader Marks 179

Strain 71
Stress 71
Style
  Abbreviations 97–103
  Active Sentences 10–15
  Articles 157–58
  Beginnings 21–23
  Bibliographies 154
  Capitalization 86–97
  Checklist 9–10
  Clarity 19–20
  Clichés 15–16
  Cold and Pompous Writing 29–34
  Conciseness 15–18
  Credit Lines 174–75
  Definition 9
  Developing Style 9–43
  Endings 23–24
  Irrelevant Information 16
  Letters and Memos 129–33
  List of Illustrations 175
  Nondiscriminatory
    Communication 114–27
  Passive Sentences 10–15
  Precise Words 24–29
  Proposals 158–60
  Publicity Releases 158, 160, 162
  Punctuation 77–86
  Reader Requirements 9
  Repetition 18
  Reports 153–57
  Shifting Voice 13
  Spelling 103–13
  Unnecessary Words 16–17
  Word Division 73–77
Stylebooks 97, 171
Subconscious 71
Subheads
  Outline Topics 166–70
  in Proposals 158–60
  in Reports 153–54
  in Table of Contents 156

Subject
  See Topics
Subject Line
  in Letters 142
Substantially 60
Subtopics
  Research 3
Suffixes and Other Word Endings
  in Compound Words 83–84
  Multiple-Syllable Words 106
  One-Syllable Words 105–6
  in Word Division 75
  Words Ending in *-ation* 107
  Words Ending in *e* 106–7
  Words Ending in *-ize, -ise, -yze*
    108
  Words Ending in *-sede, -ceed,
    -cede* 107–8
  Words Ending in *y* 108
  Words with a *c* 108
Superfluous 70
Superior Number
  Proofreader Marks 180
Supplementary 53
Supplementary Material
  in Reports 153
Suppose 63
Supposedly 69
Survey of Current Business 166
Syllabication 74–76
Syllables
  in Spelling 105–6
Syntax 62
Systematize 71
Systemize 71

Table of Contents
  in Reports 154, 156
Tables and Charts
  Captions and Legends 174
  Copyrighted Material 174–75
  Credit Lines 174–75

Format 176
List of Illustrations 174
Position in Manuscript 175
in Reports 154
Selecting 173
Source Notes and Footnotes 175
Teasers
as Introductions 22
Technical Writing
Use of Abbreviations 97, 99,
102–3
Thank You Letters 143, 144
That 71
*Thomas' Register of American
Manufacturers* 164
Though 47
Title Page
in Reports 155
Titles
Abbreviations 101
Capitalization of 92–93, 95–97
Equality Toward Sexes 124
for Women 122–24
Tokenism 117–18
Topics
Outline 5, 166–70
in Proposals 158–60
Research 3, 166–70
Topographical Names
Capitalization of 88
Toward 72
Towards 72
Trace 72
Trade Names
Capitalization of 93–94
Transitions
after Beginning 21
for Clarity 18
Punctuation 80
in Revision 7, 171
Transpire 63
Transpose
Proofreader Marks 179

Trite Expressions
List of 34–43
Troublesome Words 44–72
Spelling List 109–13
Typefaces 178
Typemarking 177–81
Typing
Articles 157–58
Manuscript 169, 177
Releases 160–61
Reports 154, 157
Statistical Matter 175
See also model letters and memos
in chapter 5

*Ulrich's International Periodicals
Directory* 164
Unabridged 45
Unconscious 71
Unilateral 51
Uninterested 57
United States
Abbreviation of 102
Unorganized 57
Unpractical 64
Unqualified 58
Unsatisfied 58
*U.S. Government Organization
Manual* 164
Usual 55

Vague Words 25
Value Line 166
Varied 72
Various 72
Verbal 67
Vessels
Capitalization of 92–93
Vestige 72
Viable 72

Vietnam Veterans Readjustment
   Act of 1974 121
Viewpoint 68
Vogue Words 32–33
   List of 32
Voice
   See Active Voice, Passive Voice
Vowels
   in Spelling 104–9

Wall Street Journal 166
Wall Street Journal Index 165
Want 65, 72
Wars
   Capitalization of 92
Well 62
Whether 63
Which 71
Whiteprint 181
Who 72
Whom 72
Widows
   in Printing 181
Will 70
Wish 72
Without Bias 115
Word Division
   Addresses 77
   Characters at the End of a Line
      75
   Contractions 76
   with Dash 77
   Double Consonants 75
   Figures 76
   Hyphenated Words 76
   Guidelines 74
   Hyphens 73–74
   One-Letter Syllables 75–76
   One-Syllable Words 74
   Prefixes and Suffixes 75
   Pronounciation 74–76
   Proper Names 76

Syllabication 74–76
Word Groups 76–77
Words of Less Than Six Letters
   74–75
Wordiness 15–18
Words
   Abbreviations 97–103
   Abstract Words 25
   Asexual Words 125
   Capitalization 86–97
   Clichés 15
   Discriminatory Language 114–
      27
   Euphemism 33
   Gobbledygook 33
   Inadequate Detail 27
   Irrelevant Information 16
   Jargon 33
   Pompous Writing 29–34
   Precise Words 24
   Prefixes 33–34, 108–9
   Prejudice 26
   Punctuation 77–86
   Repetition 18
   Simple Language 28–29
   Spelling 103–13
   Suffixes 33–34, 105–8
   Trite Expressions 34–43
   Troublesome Words 44–72,
      109–13
   Unnecessary Words 16–17, 34–
      43
   Vague Words 25
   Word Choice, 20, 44–72
   Word Division 73–77
Workable 72
Writing
   Abbreviations 97–103
   Articles 157–58
   Capitalization 86–97
   Checklist 171–72
   Drafts 5–6, 169–71, 173–77
   Essentials of 1–7

Freelancers 181–82
Letters 128–51
Marking Copy 177–78
Memos 128–51
Nondiscriminatory Writing 114–27
Organization 1–2, 166–69
Processing Proofs 178–81
Proposals 158
Publicity Releases 158–61

Punctuation 77–86
Reports 152–57
Research 3–4, 161–66
Revision 6–8, 169–73
Spelling 103–13
Stages of 1–8
Standards 8
Style 9–43
Word Choice 44–71
Word Division 73–77